MznLnx

Missing Links Exam Preps

Exam Prep for

Calculus:Concepts and Contexts

Stewart, 2nd Edition

The MznLnx Exam Prep is your link from the texbook and lecture to your exams.
The MznLnx Exam Preps are unauthorized and comprehensive reviews of your textbooks.

All material provided by MznLnx and Rico Publications (c) 2010
Textbook publishers and textbook authors do not particpate in or contribute to these reviews.

MznLnx

Rico
Publications

Exam Prep for Calculus:Concepts and Contexts
2nd Edition
Stewart

Publisher: Raymond Houge
Assistant Editor: Michael Rouger
Text and Cover Designer: Lisa Buckner
Marketing Manager: Sara Swagger
Project Manager, Editorial Production: Jerry Emerson
Art Director: Vernon Lowerui

Product Manager: Dave Mason
Editorial Assitant: Rachel Guzmanji
Pedagogy: Debra Long
Cover Image: Jim Reed/Getty Images
Text and Cover Printer: City Printing, Inc.
Compositor: Media Mix, Inc.

(c) 2010 Rico Publications

ALL RIGHTS RESERVED. No part of this work covered by the copyright may be reproduced or used in any form or by an means--graphic, electronic, or mechanical, including photocopying, recording, taping, Web distribution, information storage, and retrieval systems, or in any other manner--without the written permission of the publisher.

Printed in the United States
ISBN:

For more information about our products, contact us at:
Dave.Mason@RicoPublications.com

For permission to use material from this text or product, submit a request online to:
Dave.Mason@RicoPublications.com

Contents

CHAPTER 1
Functions and Models — 1

CHAPTER 2
Limits and Derivatives — 20

CHAPTER 3
Differentiation Rules — 31

CHAPTER 4
Applications of Differentiation — 50

CHAPTER 5
Integrals — 58

CHAPTER 6
Applications of Integration — 73

CHAPTER 7
Differential Equations — 82

CHAPTER 8
Infinite Sequences and Series — 91

CHAPTER 9
Vectors and the Geometry of Space — 104

CHAPTER 10
Vector Functions — 113

CHAPTER 11
Partial Derivatives — 121

CHAPTER 12
Multiple Integrals — 136

CHAPTER 13
Vector Calculus — 145

ANSWER KEY — 151

TO THE STUDENT

COMPREHENSIVE

The *MznLnx* Exam Prep series is designed to help you pass your exams. Editors at MznLnx review your textbooks and then prepare these practice exams to help you master the textbook material. Unlike study guides, workbooks, and practice tests provided by the texbook publisher and textbook authors, *MznLnx* gives you **all** of the material in each chapter in exam form, not just samples, so you can be sure to nail your exam.

MECHANICAL

The MznLnx Exam Prep series creates exams that will help you learn the subject matter as well as test you on your understanding. Each question is designed to help you master the concept. Just working through the exams, you gain an understanding of the subject--its a simple mechanical process that produces success.

INTEGRATED STUDY GUIDE AND REVIEW

MznLnx is not just a set of exams designed to test you, its also a comprehensive review of the subject content. Each exam question is also a review of the concept, making sure that you will get the answer correct without having to go to other sources of material. You learn as you go! Its the easiest way to pass an exam.

HUMOR

Studying can be tedious and dry. MznLnx's instructional design includes moderate humor within the exam questions on occassion, to break the tedium and revitalize the brain

Chapter 1. Functions and Models

1. In mathematics, the concept of a '_____' is used to describe the behavior of a function as its argument or input either 'gets close' to some point, or as the argument becomes arbitrarily large; or the behavior of a sequence's elements as their index increases indefinitely. Limits are used in calculus and other branches of mathematical analysis to define derivatives and continuity.

   In formulas, _____ is usually abbreviated as lim

   a. BDDC
   c. 15 theorem
   b. BIBO stability
   d. Limit

2. The _____ is a method of finding the area of a shape by inscribing inside it a sequence of polygons whose areas converge to the area of the containing shape. If the sequence is correctly constructed, the difference in area between the nth polygon and the containing shape will become arbitrarily small as n becomes large. As this difference becomes arbitrarily small, the possible values for the area of the shape are systematically 'exhausted' by the lower bound areas successively established by the sequence members.

   a. BIBO stability
   c. Method of exhaustion
   b. 15 theorem
   d. BDDC

3. In infinitesimal calculus, a _____ is traditionally an infinitesimally small change in a variable. For example, if x is a variable, then a change in the value of x is often denoted Δx (or δx when this change is considered to be small.) The _____ dx represents such a change, but is infinitely small.

   a. Related rates
   c. Dirichlet integral
   b. Continuous function
   d. Differential

4. _____, a field in mathematics, is the study of how functions change when their inputs change. The primary object of study in _____ is the derivative. A closely related notion is the differential.

   a. Stationary phase approximation
   c. Slant asymptote
   b. Differential calculus
   d. Horizontal asymptote

5. Integration is an important concept in mathematics, specifically in the field of calculus and, more broadly, mathematical analysis. Given a function f of a real variable x and an interval [a, b] of the real line, the _____

   $$\int_a^b f(x)\, dx,$$

   is defined informally to be the net signed area of the region in the xy-plane bounded by the graph of f, the x-axis, and the vertical lines x = a and x = b.

   The term '_____' may also refer to the notion of antiderivative, a function F whose derivative is the given function f.

   a. Indefinite integral
   c. Integral test for convergence
   b. Integrand
   d. Integral

6. A _____ of a curve is a line that (locally) intersects two points on the curve. The word secant comes from the Latin secare, for to cut.

It can be used to approximate the tangent to a curve, at some point P. If the secant to a curve is defined by two points, P and Q, with P fixed and Q variable, as Q approaches P along the curve, the direction of the secant approaches that of the tangent at P, assuming there is just one.

   a. Kappa curve
   b. Witch of Agnesi
   c. Curve
   d. Secant line

7. In geometry, the _____ (or simply the tangent) to a curve at a given point is the straight line that 'just touches' the curve at that point (in the sense explained more precisely below.) As it passes through the point of tangency, the _____ is 'going in the same direction' as the curve, and in this sense it is the best straight-line approximation to the curve at that point. The same definition applies to space curves and curves in n-dimensional Euclidean space.
   a. Minimal surface
   b. Sphere
   c. Lie derivative
   d. Tangent line

8. In physics, _____ is defined as the rate of change of position. it is vector physical quantity; both speed and direction are required to define it. In the SI (metric) system, it is measured in meters per second: (m/s) or ms^{-1}.
   a. 15 theorem
   b. BIBO stability
   c. BDDC
   d. Velocity

9. In mathematics, a (topological) _____ is defined as follows: let I be an interval of real numbers (i.e. a non-empty connected subset of $\mathbb{R}$); then a _____ γ is a continuous mapping $\gamma : I \to X$, where X is a topological space. The _____ γ is said to be simple if it is injective, i.e. if for all x, y in I, we have $\gamma(x) = \gamma(y) \implies x = y$. If I is a closed bounded interval $[a, b]$, we also allow the possibility $\gamma(a) = \gamma(b)$ (this convention makes it possible to talk about closed simple _____ .)
   a. Prolate cycloid
   b. Closed curve
   c. Tractrix
   d. Curve

10. _____ are a set of problems generally thought to have been devised by Zeno of Elea to support Parmenides's doctrine that 'all is one' and that, contrary to the evidence of our senses, the belief in plurality and change is mistaken, and in particular that motion is nothing but an illusion. It is usually assumed, based on Plato's Parmenides 128c-d, that Zeno took on the project of creating these paradoxes because other philosophers had created paradoxes against Parmenides's view. Thus Zeno can be interpreted as saying that to assume there is plurality is even more absurd than assuming there is only 'the One' (Parmenides 128d.)
   a. BIBO stability
   b. BDDC
   c. Zeno's paradoxes
   d. 15 theorem

11. In mathematics, a _____ is an ordered list of objects (or events). Like a set, it contains members (also called elements or terms), and the number of terms (possibly infinite) is called the length of the _____. Unlike a set, order matters, and the exact same elements can appear multiple times at different positions in the _____.
   a. Sequence
   b. 15 theorem
   c. Y-intercept
   d. BDDC

Chapter 1. Functions and Models

12. In economics, the _____ functional form of production functions is widely used to represent the relationship of an output to inputs. It was proposed by Knut Wicksell (1851-1926), and tested against statistical evidence by Charles Cobb and Paul Douglas in 1900-1928.

For production, the function is

$$Y = AL^\alpha K^\beta,$$

where:

- Y = total production (the monetary value of all goods produced in a year)
- L = labor input
- K = capital input
- A = total factor productivity
- α and β are the output elasticities of labor and capital, respectively. These values are constants determined by available technology.

Output elasticity measures the responsiveness of output to a change in levels of either labor or capital used in production, ceteris paribus. For example if α = 0.15, a 1% increase in labor would lead to approximately a 0.15% increase in output.

  a. BIBO stability
  b. Cobb-Douglas
  c. 15 theorem
  d. BDDC

13. In mathematics, a _____ (or just conic) is a curve obtained by intersecting a cone (more precisely, a circular conical surface) with a plane. A _____ is therefore a restriction of a quadric surface to the plane. The conic sections were named and studied as long ago as 200 BC, when Apollonius of Perga undertook a systematic study of their properties.
  a. 15 theorem
  b. Conic section
  c. BDDC
  d. Foci

14. In mathematics, the _____ (or replacement set) of a given function is the set of 'input' values for which the function is defined. For instance, the _____ of cosine would be all real numbers, while the _____ of the square root would be only numbers greater than or equal to 0 (ignoring complex numbers in both cases.) In a representation of a function in a xy Cartesian coordinate system, the _____ is represented on the x axis (or abscissa.)
  a. 15 theorem
  b. BDDC
  c. BIBO stability
  d. Domain

15. In geometry, a _____ is a special plane curve generated by the trace of a fixed point on a small circle that rolls within a larger circle. It is comparable to the cycloid but instead of the circle rolling along a line, it rolls within a circle. The red curve is a _____ traced as the smaller black circle rolls around inside the larger blue circle (parameters are R=3.0, r=1.0, and so k=3), giving a deltoid.

If the smaller circle has radius r, and the larger circle has radius R = kr, then the parametric equations for the curve can be given by either:

$$x(\theta) = (R - r)\cos\theta + r\cos\left(\frac{R-r}{r}\theta\right)$$
$$y(\theta) = (R - r)\sin\theta - r\sin\left(\frac{R-r}{r}\theta\right),$$

or:

$$x(\theta) = r(k-1)\cos\theta + r\cos((k-1)\theta)$$
$$y(\theta) = r(k-1)\sin\theta - r\sin((k-1)\theta).$$

If k is an integer, then the curve is closed, and has k cusps (i.e., sharp corners, where the curve is not differentiable.)

a. Hypocycloid
b. Kappa curve
c. Closed curve
d. Bullet-nose curve

16. Cantor defined two kinds of _____ numbers, the ordinal numbers and the cardinal numbers. Ordinal numbers may be identified with well-ordered sets, or counting carried on to any stopping point, including points after an _____ number have already been counted. Generalizing finite and the ordinary _____ sequences which are maps from the positive integers leads to mappings from ordinal numbers, and transfinite sequences.
    a. AUSM
    b. ACTRAN
    c. ALGOR
    d. Infinite

17. Continuous functions are of utmost importance in mathematics and applications. However, not all functions are continuous. If a function is not continuous at a point in its domain, one says that it has a _____ there. The set of all points of _____ of a function may be a discrete set, a dense set, or even the entire domain of the function.
    a. BDDC
    b. BIBO stability
    c. 15 theorem
    d. Discontinuity

18. In mathematics, the _____ of a function is the set of all 'output' values produced by that function. Sometimes it is called the image, or more precisely, the image of the domain of the function. If a function is a surjection then its _____ is equal to its codomain.
    a. Surjective
    b. Constant function
    c. Range
    d. Piecewise-defined function

19. The terms '_____' and 'independent variable' are used in similar but subtly different ways in mathematics and statistics as part of the standard terminology in those subjects. They are used to distinguish between two types of quantities being considered, separating them into those available at the start of a process and those being created by it, where the latter (dependent variables) are dependent on the former (independent variables.)

In traditional calculus, a function is defined as a relation between two terms called variables because their values vary.

    a. BIBO stability   b. 15 theorem
    c. Dependent variable   d. BDDC

20. The terms 'dependent variable' and '_____' are used in similar but subtly different ways in mathematics and statistics as part of the standard terminology in those subjects. They are used to distinguish between two types of quantities being considered, separating them into those available at the start of a process and those being created by it, where the latter (dependent variables) are dependent on the former (independent variables.)

In traditional calculus, a function is defined as a relation between two terms called variables because their values vary.

    a. AUSM   b. ALGOR
    c. ACTRAN   d. Independent variable

21. In mathematics, an _____, is the apparent shape of a circle viewed obliquely from outside it, as distinct from a hyperbola which is the shape seen from inside. It is the finite or bounded case of a conic section as a shape cut in a cone by a plane, the unbounded cases being the parabola, which like the _____ remains connected, and the hyperbola, which separates into two connected components or branches.

Equivalently an _____ can be defined as the locus of points, or path traced out, in a plane such that the sum of the distances from the moving point to two fixed points remains constant.

    a. ACTRAN   b. ALGOR
    c. AUSM   d. Ellipse

22. In mathematics, the _____ is a conic section, the intersection of a right circular conical surface and a plane parallel to a generating straight line of that surface. Given a point (the focus) and a line (the directrix) that lie in a plane, the locus of points in that plane that are equidistant to them is a _____.

A particular case arises when the plane is tangent to the conical surface of a circle.

    a. 15 theorem   b. BIBO stability
    c. BDDC   d. Parabola

23. A _____ is a type of display using Cartesian coordinates to display values for two variables for a set of data. The data is displayed as a collection of points, each having the value of one variable determining the position on the horizontal axis and the value of the other variable determining the position on the vertical axis.

    a. BDDC   b. BIBO stability
    c. 15 theorem   d. Scatter plot

24. In geometry, the _____, pronounced , are a pair of special points used in describing conic sections. The four types of conic sections are the circle, parabola, ellipse, and hyperbola.

The focus has two equivalent defining properties; and they always fall on the major axis of symmetry of the conic.

a. BDDC
b. 15 theorem
c. Latus rectum
d. Foci

25. The _____ is a test to determine if a relation or its graph is a function or not. For a relation or graph to be a function, it can have at most a single y-value for each x-value. Thus, a vertical line drawn at any x-position on the graph of a function will intersect the graph at most once.

a. 15 theorem
b. BIBO stability
c. BDDC
d. Vertical Line Test

26. In mathematics, a _____ is a function whose definition is dependent on the value of the independent variable. Mathematically, a real-valued function f of a real variable x is a relationship whose definition is given differently on disjoint subsets of its domain

The word piecewise is also used to describe any property of a _____ that holds for each piece but may not hold for the whole domain of the function.

a. Range
b. Surjective
c. Constant function
d. Piecewise-defined function

27. In mathematics, the _____ (or modulus) of a real number is its numerical value without regard to its sign. So, for example, 3 is the _____ of both 3 and −3.

The _____ of a number a is denoted by $|a|$.

a. Area hyperbolic functions
b. Absolute value
c. Exponential function
d. ACTRAN

28. The _____ are a pair of first order, non-linear, differential equations frequently used to describe the dynamics of biological systems in which two species interact, one a predator and one its prey. They were proposed independently by Alfred J. Lotka in 1925 and Vito Volterra in 1926.

where

- y is the number of some predator;
- x is the number of its prey;
- dy/dt and dx/dt represents the growth of the two populations against time;
- t represents the time; and
- >α, >β, >γ and >δ are parameters representing the interaction of the two species.

When multiplied out, the equations take a form useful for physical interpretation. Their origin should be considered from a more general framework,

where both functions represent per capita growth rates of the prey and predator, respectively.

a. BIBO stability
b. BDDC
c. Lotka-Volterra equations
d. 15 theorem

29. A _____ is an algebraic equation in which each term is either a constant or the product of a constant and (the first power of) a single variable. Linear equations can have one, two, three or more variables. Linear equations occur with great regularity in applied mathematics.
   a. BDDC
   b. 15 theorem
   c. Cubic function
   d. Linear equation

30. In mathematics, even functions and odd functions are functions which satisfy particular symmetry relations, with respect to taking additive inverses. They are important in many areas of mathematical analysis, especially the theory of power series and Fourier series. They are named for the parity of the powers of the power functions which satisfy each condition: the function $f(x) = x^n$ is an _____ if n is an even integer, and it is an odd function if n is an odd integer.
   a. Infinite series
   b. Operational calculus
   c. Integral of secant cubed
   d. Even function

31. In mathematics, even functions and odd functions are functions which satisfy particular symmetry relations, with respect to taking additive inverses. They are important in many areas of mathematical analysis, especially the theory of power series and Fourier series. They are named for the parity of the powers of the power functions which satisfy each condition: the function $f(x) = x^n$ is an even function if n is an even integer, and it is an _____ if n is an odd integer.
   a. Even function
   b. Integral of secant cubed
   c. Integration by substitution
   d. Odd function

32. In mathematics, a function on the real numbers is called a _____ (or staircase function) if it can be written as a finite linear combination of indicator functions of intervals. Informally speaking, a _____ is a piecewise constant function having only finitely many pieces.

a. Hyperbolic sine
b. Multiplicative inverse
c. Hyperbolic tangent
d. Step function

33. _____ generally conveys two primary meanings. The first is an imprecise sense of harmonious or aesthetically-pleasing proportionality and balance; such that it reflects beauty or perfection. The second meaning is a precise and well-defined concept of balance or 'patterned self-similarity' that can be demonstrated or proved according to the rules of a formal system: by geometry, through physics or otherwise.
   a. BIBO stability
   b. BDDC
   c. Symmetry
   d. 15 theorem

34. In mathematics, a _____ is a function which preserves the given order. This concept first arose in calculus, and was later generalized to the more abstract setting of order theory.

In calculus, a function f defined on a subset of the real numbers with real values is called monotonic (also monotonically increasing or non-decreasing), if for all x and y such that x >≤ y one has f(x) >≤ f(y), so f preserves the order.

   a. Pettis integral
   b. 15 theorem
   c. Monotonic function
   d. Pseudo-differential operator

35. A _____ or Gompertz function, named after Benjamin Gompertz, is a sigmoid function. It is a type of mathematical model for a time series, where growth is slowest at the start and end of a time period. Graphs of Gompertz curves, showing the effect of varying one of a,b,c while keeping the others constant.

$$y(t) = ae^{be^{ct}}$$

where

- a is the upper asymptote
- c is the growth rate
- b, c are negative numbers
- e is Euler's Number (e = 2.71828...)

The function curve can be derived from Gompertz's law, which states the rate of mortality (decay) falls exponentially with current size. Mathematically

$$k^r \propto \frac{1}{y(t)}$$

where

- $r = \dfrac{y'(t)}{y(t)}$ is the rate of growth.
- k is an arbitrary constant.

Examples of uses for Gompertz curves include:

- Mobile phone uptake, where costs were initially high (so uptake was slow), followed by a period of rapid growth, followed by a slowing of uptake as saturation was reached.
- Population in a confined space, as birth rates first increase and then slow as resource limits are reached.
- Modeling of growth of tumors

In the sixties A.K. Laird for the first time successfully used the _____ to fit data of growth of tumors. In fact, tumors are cellular populations growing in a confined space where the availability of nutrients is limited.

a. Spheroidal wave functions
b. Duffing equation
c. Gompertz curve
d. Neumann-Dirichlet method

36. In statistics, given a (random) sample $(Y_i, X_{i1}, \ldots, X_{ip})$, $i = 1, \ldots, n$ the most general form of _____ is formulated as

$$Y_i = \beta_0 + \beta_1 \phi_1(X_{i1}) + \ldots + \beta_p \phi_p(X_{ip}) + \varepsilon_i \qquad i = 1, \ldots, n$$

where $\phi_1, \ldots, \phi_p$ may be nonlinear functions.

In matrix notation this model can be written as

$$Y = X\beta + \varepsilon$$

where Y is an n × 1 column vector, X is an n × (p + 1) matrix, β is a (p + 1) × 1 vector of (unobservable) parameters, and ε is an n × 1 vector of errors, which are uncorrelated random variables each with expected value 0 and variance σ^2. Note that depending on the context the sample can be seen as fixed (observable), or random.

a. 15 theorem
b. Linear model
c. BDDC
d. BIBO stability

37. _____ is finding a curve which has the best fit to a series of data points and possibly other constraints. This section is an introduction to both interpolation (where an exact fit to constraints is expected) and regression analysis. Both are sometimes used for extrapolation.

a. Series acceleration
b. Propagation of uncertainty
c. Curve fitting
d. Well-posed problem

38. In mathematics, _____ is the process of constructing new data points outside a discrete set of known data points. It is similar to the process of interpolation, which constructs new points between known points, but the results of extrapolations are often less meaningful, and are subject to greater uncertainty. Example illustration of the _____ problem, consisting of assigning a meaningful value at the blue box, at x = 7, given the red data points.

A sound choice of which _____ method to apply relies on a prior knowledge of the process that created the existing data points.

a. ALGOR
b. ACTRAN
c. AUSM
d. Extrapolation

39. In statistics, _____ is a form of regression analysis in which the relationship between one or more independent variables and another variable, called dependent variable, is modeled by a least squares function, called _____ equation. This function is a linear combination of one or more model parameters, called regression coefficients. A _____ equation with one independent variable represents a straight line.

a. Standard deviation
b. Poisson distribution
c. Normal distribution
d. Linear regression

40. The method of _____ or ordinary _____ is used to solve overdetermined systems. _____ is often applied in statistical contexts, particularly regression analysis.

_____ can be interpreted as a method of fitting data. The best fit in the _____ sense is that instance of the model for which the sum of squared residuals has its least value, a residual being the difference between an observed value and the value given by the model.

a. 15 theorem
b. Least squares
c. BIBO stability
d. BDDC

41. In mathematics, a _____ is a constant multiplicative factor of a certain object. For example, in the expression $9x^2$, the _____ of x^2 is 9.

The object can be such things as a variable, a vector, a function, etc.

a. Leading coefficient
b. Degree of the polynomial
c. Difference polynomial
d. Coefficient

42. In mathematics, a _____ is a function of the form

$$f(x) = ax^3 + bx^2 + cx + d,$$

where a is nonzero; or in other words, a polynomial of degree three. The derivative of a _____ is a quadratic function. The integral of a _____ is a quartic function.

a. Cubic function
b. BDDC
c. Linear equation
d. 15 theorem

43. When a polynomial is expressed as a sum or difference of terms (e.g., in standard or canonical form), the exponent of the term with the highest exponent is the _____. The degree of a term is the sum of the powers of each variable in the term. The words degree and order are used interchangeably.

Chapter 1. Functions and Models

a. Degree of the polynomial
c. Sheffer sequence

b. Coefficient
d. Quadratic function

44. A _____, in mathematics, is a polynomial function of the form $f(x) = ax^2 + bx + c$, where $a \neq 0$. The graph of a _____ is a parabola whose major axis is parallel to the y-axis.

The expression ax² + bx + c in the definition of a _____ is a polynomial of degree 2 or a 2nd degree polynomial, because the highest exponent of x is 2.

a. Coefficient
c. Constant term

b. Degree of the polynomial
d. Quadratic function

45. In mathematics, an _____ is informally a function which satisfies a polynomial equation whose coefficients are themselves polynomials. For example, an _____ in one variable x is a solution y for an equation

$$a_n(x)y^n + a_{n-1}(x)y^{n-1} + \cdots + a_0(x) = 0$$

where the coefficients $a_i(x)$ are polynomial functions of x. A function which is not algebraic is called a transcendental function.

a. Algebraic function
c. ALGOR

b. ACTRAN
d. AUSM

46. In calculus, an _____ is the limit of a definite integral as an endpoint of the interval of integration approaches either a specified real number or ∞ or −∞ or, in some cases, as both endpoints approach limits.

Specifically, an _____ is a limit of the form

$$\lim_{b \to \infty} \int_a^b f(x)\, dx, \qquad \lim_{a \to -\infty} \int_a^b f(x)\, dx,$$

or of the form

$$\lim_{c \to b^-} \int_a^c f(x)\, dx, \qquad \lim_{c \to a^+} \int_c^b f(x)\, dx,$$

in which one takes a limit in one or the other (or sometimes both) endpoints . Improper integrals may also occur at an interior point of the domain of integration, or at multiple such points.

a. AUSM
c. Improper integral

b. ACTRAN
d. ALGOR

47. In mathematics, a _____ is any function which can be written as the ratio of two polynomial functions.

$$y = \frac{x^2 - 3x - 2}{x^2 - 4}$$

In the case of one variable, x, a _____ is a function of the form

$$f(x) = \frac{P(x)}{Q(x)}$$

where P and Q are polynomial function in x and Q is not the zero polynomial. The domain of f is the set of all points x for which the denominator Q(x) is not zero.

a. BIBO stability
b. BDDC
c. Rational function
d. 15 theorem

48. In mathematics, a _____ or reciprocal for a number x, denoted by $1/x$ or x^{-1}, is a number which when multiplied by x yields the multiplicative identity, 1. The _____ of x is also called the reciprocal of x. The _____ of a fraction p/q is q/p.
 a. Square root function
 b. Heaviside step function
 c. Hyperbolic sine
 d. Multiplicative inverse

49. Trigonometry is a branch of mathematics that deals with triangles, particularly those plane triangles in which one angle has 90 degrees (right triangles.) Trigonometry deals with relationships between the sides and the angles of triangles and with the _____ functions, which describe those relationships.

Trigonometry has applications in both pure mathematics and in applied mathematics, where it is essential in many branches of science and technology.

 a. 15 theorem
 b. Trigonometric functions
 c. Trigonometric integrals
 d. Trigonometric

50. In mathematics, the _____ are functions of an angle. They are important in the study of triangles and modeling periodic phenomena, among many other applications. _____ are commonly defined as ratios of two sides of a right triangle containing the angle, and can equivalently be defined as the lengths of various line segments from a unit circle.
 a. Trigonometric
 b. 15 theorem
 c. Trigonometric integrals
 d. Trigonometric functions

51. The _____ is a function in mathematics. The application of this function to a value x is written as exp(x). Equivalently, this can be written in the form e^x, where e is a mathematical constant, the base of the natural logarithm, which equals approximately 2.718281828, and is also known as Euler's number.
 a. Integral part
 b. Exponential function
 c. ACTRAN
 d. Area hyperbolic functions

Chapter 1. Functions and Models

52. The function log_b(x) depends on both b and x, but the term _____ in standard usage refers to a function of the form log_b(x) in which the base b is fixed and so the only argument is x. Thus there is one _____ for each value of the base b (which must be positive and must differ from 1.) Viewed in this way, the base-b _____ is the inverse function of the exponential function b^x.

  a. BIBO stability
  b. BDDC
  c. 15 theorem
  d. Logarithm function

53. A _____ is a function that does not satisfy a polynomial equation whose coefficients are themselves polynomials, in contrast to an algebraic function, which does satisfy such an equation. In other words a _____ is a function which 'transcends' algebra in the sense that it cannot be expressed in terms of a finite sequence of the algebraic operations of addition, multiplication, and root extraction.

Examples of transcendental functions include the exponential function, the logarithm, and the trigonometric functions.

  a. BDDC
  b. Transcendental function
  c. 15 theorem
  d. BIBO stability

54. In calculus, an antiderivative, primitive or _____ of a function f is a function F whose derivative is equal to f, i.e., F ' = f. The process of solving for antiderivatives is antidifferentiation (or indefinite integration.) Antiderivatives are related to definite integrals through the fundamental theorem of calculus: the definite integral of a function over an interval is equal to the difference between the values of an antiderivative evaluated at the endpoints of the interval.

  a. Integration by parts operator
  b. Indefinite integral
  c. Arc length
  d. Integral test for convergence

55. A _____ is a model used within physics to explain how gravity exists in the universe. In its original concept, gravity was a force between point masses. Following Newton, Laplace attempted to model gravity as some kind of radiation field or fluid, and since the 19th century explanations for gravity have usually been sought in terms of a field model, rather than a point attraction.

  a. 15 theorem
  b. BDDC
  c. BIBO stability
  d. Gravitational field

56. The _____, H, also called the unit step function, is a discontinuous function whose value is zero for negative argument and one for positive argument. It seldom matters what value is used for H, since H is mostly used as a distribution. The function is used in the mathematics of control theory and signal processing to represent a signal that switches on at a specified time and stays switched on indefinitely.

  a. Hyperbolic functions
  b. Hyperbolic cosine
  c. Signum function
  d. Heaviside step function

57. The _____ is an elementary unary real function, easily computable as the mean of its independent variable and its absolute value.

This function is applied in engineering (e.g., in the theory of DSP.) The name _____ can be derived by the look of its graph.

a. Ramp function
b. Bounded function
c. Differential calculus
d. Monodromy

58. In geometry, an _____ is a plane curve produced by tracing the path of a chosen point of a circle -- called epicycle -- which rolls without slipping around a fixed circle. It is a particular kind of roulette.

If the smaller circle has radius r, and the larger circle has radius R = kr, then the parametric equations for the curve can be given by either:

$$x(\theta) = (R+r)\cos\theta - r\cos\left(\frac{R+r}{r}\theta\right)$$
$$y(\theta) = (R+r)\sin\theta - r\sin\left(\frac{R+r}{r}\theta\right),$$

or:

$$x(\theta) = r(k+1)\cos\theta - r\cos((k+1)\theta)$$
$$y(\theta) = r(k+1)\sin\theta - r\sin((k+1)\theta).$$

If k is an integer, then the curve is closed, and has k cusps (i.e., sharp corners, where the curve is not differentiable.)

a. ALGOR
b. Asymptotic curve
c. ACTRAN
d. Epicycloid

59. In mathematics, a _____ is a unicursal quartic curve with three inflection points, given by the equation

$$a^2 y^2 - b^2 x^2 = x^2 y^2$$

The bullet curve has three double points in the real projective plane, at x=0 and y=0, x=0 and z=0, and y=0 and z=0, and is therefore a unicursal (rational) curve of genus zero.

If

$$f(z) = \sum_{n=0}^{\infty} \binom{2n}{n} z^{2n+1} = z + 2z^3 + 6z^5 + 20z^7 + \cdots$$

then

$$y = f\left(\frac{x}{2a}\right) \pm 2b$$

are the two branches of the bullet curve at the origin.

a. Closed curve
b. Folium of Descartes
c. Hypocycloid
d. Bullet-nose curve

60. A _____ is a mathematical equation for an unknown function of one or several variables that relates the values of the function itself and of its derivatives of various orders. they play a prominent role in engineering, physics, economics and other disciplines.

A simplified real world example of a _____ is modeling the acceleration of a ball falling through the air (considering only gravity and air resistance.)

a. Petrovsky lacuna
b. Lax pair
c. Differential equation
d. Structural stability

61. The _____ of a quantity whose value decreases with time is the interval required for the quantity to decay to half of its initial value. The concept originated in describing how long it takes atoms to undergo radioactive decay but also applies in a wide variety of other situations.

The term '_____' dates to 1907.

a. 15 theorem
b. BIBO stability
c. BDDC
d. Half-life

62. In mathematics, the _____ of a function y = f(x) is a function that, in some fashion, 'undoes' the effect of f The _____ of f is denoted f^{-1}. The statements y=f(x) and x=f^{-1}(y) are equivalent.

a. ACTRAN
b. Inverse
c. AUSM
d. ALGOR

63. In mathematics, the _____ is a test used to determine if a function is injective, surjective or bijective.

Suppose there is a function f : X → Y with a graph., and you have a horizontal line of X x Y :

$$y_0 \in Y, \{(x, y_0) : x \in X\} = (X \times y_0)$$

- If the function is injective, then it can be visualized as one whose graph is never intersected by any horizontal line more than once.
- If and only if f is surjective, any horizontal line will intersect the graph at least at one point (when the horizontal line is in the codomain.)
- If f is bijective, any horizontal line will intersect the graph at exactly one point.

This test is also used to find whether or not the inverse of the function is indeed a function as well. This is due to the reflective properties of the function over y=x.

Chapter 1. Functions and Models

a. 15 theorem
b. BIBO stability
c. BDDC
d. Horizontal Line Test

64. An injective function is called an injection, and is also said to be a _____ function (not to be confused with _____ correspondence, i.e. a bijective function.)

A function f that is not injective is sometimes called many-to-one. (However, this terminology is also sometimes used to mean 'single-valued', i.e. each argument is mapped to at most one value.)

a. Injective function
b. One-to-one function
c. One-to-one
d. Onto

65. An injective function is called an injection, and is also said to be a _____ (not to be confused with one-to-one correspondence, i.e. a bijective function.)

A function f that is not injective is sometimes called many-to-one. (However, this terminology is also sometimes used to mean 'single-valued', i.e. each argument is mapped to at most one value.)

a. Onto
b. Injective function
c. One-to-one
d. One-to-one function

66. In vector calculus, the _____ is shorthand for either the _____ matrix or its determinant, the _____ determinant.

In algebraic geometry the _____ of a curve means the _____ variety: a group variety associated to the curve, in which the curve can be embedded.

These concepts are all named after the mathematician Carl Gustav Jacob Jacobi.

a. Contact
b. Partial derivative
c. Symmetry of second derivatives
d. Jacobian

67. The _____ of a material is defined as its mass per unit volume. The symbol of _____ is ρ '>rho.)

Mathematically:

$$d = \frac{m}{V}$$

where:

d is the _____,
m is the mass,
V is the volume.

a. BIBO stability
b. 15 theorem
c. Density
d. BDDC

68. In mathematics, _____ are a method of defining a curve. A simple kinematical example is when one uses a time parameter to determine the position, velocity, and other information about a body in motion.

Abstractly, a relation is given in the form of an equation, and it is shown also to be the image of functions from items such as R^n.

a. Parametric equations
b. Multivariable calculus
c. Laplace operator
d. Differential operator

69. In calculus, a branch of mathematics, the _____ is a measurement of how a function changes when its input changes. Loosely speaking, a _____ can be thought of as how much a quantity is changing at some given point. For example, the _____ of the position (or distance) of a vehicle with respect to time is the instantaneous velocity (respectively, instantaneous speed) at which the vehicle is traveling.

The process of finding a _____ is called differentiation. The fundamental theorem of calculus states that differentiation is the reverse process to integration.

a. Ramp function
b. Concave upwards
c. Mountain pass theorem
d. Derivative

70. In mathematics, a _____ is the graph of the system of parametric equations

$$x = A\sin(at + \delta), \quad y = B\sin(bt),$$

which describes complex harmonic motion. This family of curves was investigated by Nathaniel Bowditch in 1815, and later in more detail by Jules Antoine Lissajous in 1857.

The appearance of the figure is highly sensitive to the ratio a/b.

a. Lissajous curve
b. BIBO stability
c. 15 theorem
d. BDDC

71. In the mathematical field of numerical analysis, a _____ is a parametric curve important in computer graphics and related fields. Generalizations of Bezier curves to higher dimensions are called Bezier surfaces, of which the Bezier triangle is a special case.

Bezier curves were widely publicized in 1962 by the French engineer Pierre B>ézier, who used them to design automobile bodies.

a. 15 theorem
b. Bezier curve
c. BIBO stability
d. BDDC

72. A _____ is the curve defined by the path of a point on the edge of circular wheel as the wheel rolls along a straight line. It is an example of a roulette, a curve generated by a curve rolling on another curve.

The _____ is the solution to the brachistochrone problem (i.e. it is the curve of fastest descent under gravity) and the related tautochrone problem (i.e. the period of a ball rolling back and forth inside it does not depend on the ball's starting position.)

a. Curtate cycloid
b. Prolate cycloid
c. Tractrix
d. Cycloid

73. A _____ is the curve between two points that is covered in the least time by a body that starts at the first point with zero speed and is constrained to move along the curve to the second point, under the action of constant gravity and assuming no friction.

Given two points A and B, with A not lower than B, there is just one upside down cycloid that passes through A with infinite slope, passes also through B and does not have maximum points between A and B. This particular inverted cycloid is a _____. The curve does not depend on the body's mass or on the strength of the gravitational constant.

a. Closed curve
b. Space curve
c. Prolate cycloid
d. Brachistochrone curve

74. A tautochrone or isochrone curve is the curve for which the time taken by an object sliding without friction in uniform gravity to its lowest point is independent of its starting point. The curve is a cycloid, and the time is equal to >π times the square root of the radius over the acceleration of gravity.

The _____, the attempt to identify this curve, was solved by Christiaan Huygens in 1659. He proved geometrically in his Horologium oscillatorium (The Pendulum Clock, 1673) that the curve was a cycloid. This solution was later used to attack the problem of the brachistochrone curve. Jakob Bernoulli solved the problem using calculus in a paper (Acta Eruditorum, 1690) that saw the first published use of the term integral.

a. Space curve
b. Folium of Descartes
c. Hypocycloid
d. Tautochrone problem

75. _____ is the word created by Gilles de Roberval for the curve described by a fixed point as a circle rolls along a straight line. As a circle of radius a rolls without slipping along a line L, the center C moves parallel to L, and every other point P in the rotating plane rigidly attached to the circle traces the curve called the _____. Let CP = b. If P lies inside the circle (b < a), on its circumference (b = a), or outside (b > a), the _____ is described as being curtate, common, or prolate, respectively.

a. Hypocycloid
b. Kappa curve
c. Witch of Agnesi
d. Trochoid

76. In mathematics, an _____ is a particular type of curve: a hypocycloid with four cusps. Astroids are also superellipses: all astroids are scaled versions of the curve specified by the equation

$$x^{2/3} + y^{2/3} = 1$$

Its modern name comes from the Greek word for 'star'.

a. Epicycloid
b. ACTRAN
c. ALGOR
d. Astroid

77. In mathematics, the _____ , is the curve defined as follows.

Starting with a fixed circle, a point O on the circle is chosen. For any other point A on the circle, the secant line OA is drawn. The point M is diametrically opposite O. The line OA intersects the tangent at M at the point N. The line parallel to OM through N, and the line perpendicular to OM through A intersect at P. As the point A is varied, the path of P is the witch.

a. Closed curve
b. Cochleoid
c. Folium of Descartes
d. Witch of Agnesi

78. In mathematics, the simplest case of _____ refers to the study of problems in which one seeks to minimize or maximize a real function by systematically choosing the values of real or integer variables from within an allowed set. This (a scalar real valued objective function) is actually a small subset of this field which comprises a large area of applied mathematics and generalizes to study of means to obtain 'best available' values of some objective function given a defined domain where the elaboration is on the types of functions and the conditions and nature of the objects in the problem domain.

The first _____ technique, which is known as steepest descent, goes back to Gauss.

a. ACTRAN
b. Optimization
c. AUSM
d. ALGOR

79. _____ is a method of mathematical proof typically used to establish that a given statement is true of all natural numbers. It is done by proving that the first statement in the infinite sequence of statements is true, and then proving that if any one statement in the infinite sequence of statements is true, then so is the next one.

The method can be extended to prove statements about more general well-founded structures, such as trees; this generalization, known as structural induction, is used in mathematical logic and computer science.

a. BIBO stability
b. BDDC
c. 15 theorem
d. Mathematical Induction

Chapter 2. Limits and Derivatives

1. The _____ of an object is the extra energy which it possesses due to its motion. It is defined as the work needed to accelerate a body of a given mass from rest to its current velocity. Having gained this energy during its acceleration, the body maintains this _____ unless its speed changes.
   a. 15 theorem
   b. Kinetic energy
   c. Potential energy
   d. BDDC

2. In calculus, a _____ is either of the two limits of a function f(x) of a real variable x as x approaches a specified point either from below or from above. One should write either:

$$\lim_{x \to a^+} f(x) \text{ or } \lim_{x \downarrow a} f(x)$$

for the limit as x decreases in value approaching a (x approaches a 'from above' or 'from the right'), and similarly

$$\lim_{x \to a^-} f(x) \text{ or } \lim_{x \uparrow a} f(x)$$

for the limit as x increases in value approaching a (x approaches a 'from below' or 'from the left'.)

The two one-sided limits exist and are equal if and only if the limit of f(x) as x approaches a exists.

   a. One-sided limit
   b. AUSM
   c. ACTRAN
   d. ALGOR

3. In infinitesimal calculus, a _____ is traditionally an infinitesimally small change in a variable. For example, if x is a variable, then a change in the value of x is often denoted Δx (or δx when this change is considered to be small.) The _____ dx represents such a change, but is infinitely small.
   a. Continuous function
   b. Related rates
   c. Dirichlet integral
   d. Differential

4. A _____ is a mathematical equation for an unknown function of one or several variables that relates the values of the function itself and of its derivatives of various orders. they play a prominent role in engineering, physics, economics and other disciplines.

   A simplified real world example of a _____ is modeling the acceleration of a ball falling through the air (considering only gravity and air resistance.)

   a. Petrovsky lacuna
   b. Lax pair
   c. Differential equation
   d. Structural stability

5. Continuous functions are of utmost importance in mathematics and applications. However, not all functions are continuous. If a function is not continuous at a point in its domain, one says that it has a _____ there. The set of all points of _____ of a function may be a discrete set, a dense set, or even the entire domain of the function.
   a. BIBO stability
   b. BDDC
   c. 15 theorem
   d. Discontinuity

Chapter 2. Limits and Derivatives

6. In mathematics, the concept of a '_____' is used to describe the behavior of a function as its argument or input either 'gets close' to some point, or as the argument becomes arbitrarily large; or the behavior of a sequence's elements as their index increases indefinitely. Limits are used in calculus and other branches of mathematical analysis to define derivatives and continuity.

In formulas, _____ is usually abbreviated as lim

   a. BIBO stability
   c. Limit
   b. 15 theorem
   d. BDDC

7. Integration is an important concept in mathematics, specifically in the field of calculus and, more broadly, mathematical analysis. Given a function f of a real variable x and an interval [a, b] of the real line, the _____

$$\int_a^b f(x)\,dx,$$

is defined informally to be the net signed area of the region in the xy-plane bounded by the graph of f, the x-axis, and the vertical lines x = a and x = b.

The term '_____' may also refer to the notion of antiderivative, a function F whose derivative is the given function f.

   a. Integral
   c. Indefinite integral
   b. Integral test for convergence
   d. Integrand

8. The _____ is a method of finding the area of a shape by inscribing inside it a sequence of polygons whose areas converge to the area of the containing shape. If the sequence is correctly constructed, the difference in area between the nth polygon and the containing shape will become arbitrarily small as n becomes large. As this difference becomes arbitrarily small, the possible values for the area of the shape are systematically 'exhausted' by the lower bound areas successively established by the sequence members.

   a. Method of exhaustion
   c. BIBO stability
   b. BDDC
   d. 15 theorem

9. In mathematics and computer science, the floor and ceiling functions map a real number to the next smallest or next largest integer. More precisely, floor(x) is the largest integer not greater than x and ceiling(x) is the smallest integer not less than x.

The _____ is also called the greatest integer or entier function, and the floor of a nonnegative x may be called the integral part or integral value of x. Computer languages (other than APL) commonly use ENTIER(x) (Algol), floor(x), or int(x) (C and C++).

   a. Hyperbolic tangent
   c. Floor function
   b. Hyperbolic functions
   d. Signum function

10. In calculus, the _____ is a theorem regarding the limit of a function.

The _____ is a technical result which is very important in proofs in calculus and mathematical analysis. It is typically used to confirm the limit of a function via comparison with two other functions whose limits are known or easily computed.

a. Limit of a sequence
b. 15 theorem
c. Table of limits
d. Squeeze Theorem

11. In economics, the _____ functional form of production functions is widely used to represent the relationship of an output to inputs. It was proposed by Knut Wicksell (1851-1926), and tested against statistical evidence by Charles Cobb and Paul Douglas in 1900-1928.

For production, the function is

$$Y = AL^{\alpha}K^{\beta},$$

where:

- Y = total production (the monetary value of all goods produced in a year)
- L = labor input
- K = capital input
- A = total factor productivity
- α and β are the output elasticities of labor and capital, respectively. These values are constants determined by available technology.

Output elasticity measures the responsiveness of output to a change in levels of either labor or capital used in production, ceteris paribus. For example if $\alpha = 0.15$, a 1% increase in labor would lead to approximately a 0.15% increase in output.

a. BDDC
b. Cobb-Douglas
c. 15 theorem
d. BIBO stability

12. In mathematics, a _____ is a function for which, intuitively, small changes in the input result in small changes in the output. Otherwise, a function is said to be discontinuous. A _____ with a continuous inverse function is called bicontinuous. An intuitive though imprecise (and inexact) idea of continuity is given by the common statement that a _____ is a function whose graph can be drawn without lifting the chalk from the blackboard.

a. Leibniz function
b. Dirichlet integral
c. Continuous function
d. Maxima

13. Cantor defined two kinds of _____ numbers, the ordinal numbers and the cardinal numbers. Ordinal numbers may be identified with well-ordered sets, or counting carried on to any stopping point, including points after an _____ number have already been counted. Generalizing finite and the ordinary _____ sequences which are maps from the positive integers leads to mappings from ordinal numbers, and transfinite sequences.

a. ACTRAN	b. AUSM
c. ALGOR	d. Infinite

14. In mathematics, a _____ is any function which can be written as the ratio of two polynomial functions.

$$y = \frac{x^2 - 3x - 2}{x^2 - 4}$$

In the case of one variable, x, a _____ is a function of the form

$$f(x) = \frac{P(x)}{Q(x)}$$

where P and Q are polynomial function in x and Q is not the zero polynomial. The domain of f is the set of all points x for which the denominator Q(x) is not zero.

a. BDDC	b. BIBO stability
c. 15 theorem	d. Rational function

15. The _____ is the derived unit of energy in the International System of Units. It is defined as:

$$1\,\text{J} = 1\,\text{kg} \cdot \text{m}^2 \cdot \text{s}^{-2}$$

One _____ is the amount of energy required to perform the following physical actions:

- The work done by a force of one newton travelling through a distance of one metre;
- The work required to move an electric charge of one coulomb through an electrical potential difference of one volt; or one coulomb volt, with the symbol CÂ·V;
- The work done to produce the power of one watt continuously for one second; or one watt second (compare kilowatt hour), with the symbol WÂ·s. Thus a kilowatt hour is 3,600,000 joules or 3.6 megajoules;

1 _____ is equal to:

- 1×10^7 ergs (exactly)
- 1.6022×10^{19} eV (electronvolts)
- 0.2390 cal (gram calories or small calories)
- 2.3901×10^{-4} kcal (kilocalories, kilogram calories, large calories or food calories)
- 9.4782×10^{-4} BTU (British thermal unit)
- 0.7376 ft·lbf (foot-pound force)
- 23.7 ft·pdl (foot-poundals)
- 2.7778×10^{-7} kilowatt-hour
- 2.7778×10^{-4} watt-hour
- 9.8692×10^{-3} litre-atmosphere
- 1×10^{-44} Foe (exactly)

Units defined in terms of the _____ include:

- 1 thermochemical calorie = 4.184 J
- 1 International Table calorie = 4.1868 J
- 1 watt hour = 3600 J
- 1 kilowatt hour = 3.6×10^6 J (or 3.6 MJ)
- 1 ton TNT exploding = 4.184 GJ

Useful to remember:

- 1 _____ = 1 newton × 1 meter = 1 watt × 1 second

One _____ in everyday life is approximately:

- the energy required to lift a small apple one metre straight up.
- the energy released when that same apple falls one meter to the ground.
- the energy released as heat by a quiet person, every hundredth of a second.
- the energy required to heat one gram of dry, cool air by 1 degree Celsius.
- one hundredth of the energy a person can receive by drinking a drop of beer.
- the kinetic energy of an adult human moving a distance of about a handspan every second.

- Conversion of units
- Orders of magnitude (energy)
- Fluence

Chapter 2. Limits and Derivatives

a. BDDC
c. BIBO stability
b. 15 theorem
d. Joule

16. An _____ of a real-valued function y = f(x) is a curve which describes the behavior of f as either x or y tends to infinity.

In other words, as one moves along the graph of f(x) in some direction, the distance between it and the _____ eventually becomes smaller than any distance that one may specify.

a. ALGOR
c. ACTRAN
b. AUSM
d. Asymptote

17. The line x = a is a _____ of a curve y=f(x) if at least one of the following statements is true:

1. $\lim_{x \to a} f(x) = \pm\infty$
2. $\lim_{x \to a^-} f(x) = \pm\infty$
3. $\lim_{x \to a^+} f(x) = \pm\infty$

Intuitively, if x = a is an asymptote of f, then, if we imagine x approaching a from one side, the value of f(x) grows without bound; i.e., f(x) becomes large (positively or negatively), and, in fact, becomes larger than any finite value.

Note that f(x) may or may not be defined at a: what the function is doing precisely at x = a does not affect the asymptote. For example, consider the function

$$f(x) = \begin{cases} \frac{1}{x} & \text{if } x > 0, \\ 5 & \text{if } x \leq 0 \end{cases}$$

As $\lim_{x \to 0^+} f(x) = \infty$, f(x) has a _____ at 0, even though f(0) = 5.

Another example is $f(x) = 1/(x-1)$ which has a _____ of x=1 as shown by the limit

$$\lim_{x \to 1^+} \frac{1}{x-1} = \infty$$

In the graph of $f(x) = x + \frac{1}{x}$, the y-axis (x = 0) and the line y = x are both asymptotes.

When a linear asymptote is not parallel to the x- or y-axis, it is called either an oblique asymptote or equivalently a slant asymptote.

a. Semi-differentiability
b. Geometric function theory
c. Fractional calculus
d. Vertical asymptote

18. The _____ of a material is defined as its mass per unit volume. The symbol of _____ is ρ '>rho.)

Mathematically:

$$d = \frac{m}{V}$$

where:

d is the _____,
m is the mass,
V is the volume.

a. Density
b. BDDC
c. BIBO stability
d. 15 theorem

19. Suppose f is a function. Then the line y = a is a _____ for f if

$$\lim_{x \to \infty} f(x) = a \text{ or } \lim_{x \to -\infty} f(x) = a.$$

Intuitively, this means that f(x) can be made as close as desired to a by making x big enough. How big is big enough depends on how close one wishes to make f(x) to a.

a. Horizontal asymptote
b. Vertical asymptote
c. Bounded function
d. Mountain pass theorem

20. The _____ is a function in mathematics. The application of this function to a value x is written as exp(x). Equivalently, this can be written in the form e^x, where e is a mathematical constant, the base of the natural logarithm, which equals approximately 2.718281828, and is also known as Euler's number.

a. Integral part
b. ACTRAN
c. Exponential function
d. Area hyperbolic functions

21. In geometry, the _____ (or simply the tangent) to a curve at a given point is the straight line that 'just touches' the curve at that point (in the sense explained more precisely below.) As it passes through the point of tangency, the _____ is 'going in the same direction' as the curve, and in this sense it is the best straight-line approximation to the curve at that point. The same definition applies to space curves and curves in n-dimensional Euclidean space.

a. Sphere
b. Tangent line
c. Lie derivative
d. Minimal surface

Chapter 2. Limits and Derivatives

22. In mathematics, a (topological) _____ is defined as follows: let I be an interval of real numbers (i.e. a non-empty connected subset of $\mathbb{R}$); then a _____ γ is a continuous mapping $\gamma : I \to X$, where X is a topological space. The _____ γ is said to be simple if it is injective, i.e. if for all x, y in I, we have $\gamma(x) = \gamma(y) \implies x = y$. If I is a closed bounded interval $[a, b]$, we also allow the possibility $\gamma(a) = \gamma(b)$ (this convention makes it possible to talk about closed simple _____.)

   a. Closed curve   b. Tractrix
   c. Prolate cycloid   d. Curve

23. In physics, _____ is defined as the rate of change of position. it is vector physical quantity; both speed and direction are required to define it. In the SI (metric) system, it is measured in meters per second: (m/s) or ms^{-1}.

   a. 15 theorem   b. BDDC
   c. Velocity   d. BIBO stability

24. In mathematics, the simplest case of _____ refers to the study of problems in which one seeks to minimize or maximize a real function by systematically choosing the values of real or integer variables from within an allowed set. This (a scalar real valued objective function) is actually a small subset of this field which comprises a large area of applied mathematics and generalizes to study of means to obtain 'best available' values of some objective function given a defined domain where the elaboration is on the types of functions and the conditions and nature of the objects in the problem domain.

The first _____ technique, which is known as steepest descent, goes back to Gauss.

   a. AUSM   b. ALGOR
   c. Optimization   d. ACTRAN

25. In calculus, a branch of mathematics, the _____ is a measurement of how a function changes when its input changes. Loosely speaking, a _____ can be thought of as how much a quantity is changing at some given point. For example, the _____ of the position (or distance) of a vehicle with respect to time is the instantaneous velocity (respectively, instantaneous speed) at which the vehicle is traveling.

The process of finding a _____ is called differentiation. The fundamental theorem of calculus states that differentiation is the reverse process to integration.

   a. Concave upwards   b. Mountain pass theorem
   c. Derivative   d. Ramp function

26. In mathematics, the _____ (or replacement set) of a given function is the set of 'input' values for which the function is defined. For instance, the _____ of cosine would be all real numbers, while the _____ of the square root would be only numbers greater than or equal to 0 (ignoring complex numbers in both cases.) In a representation of a function in a xy Cartesian coordinate system, the _____ is represented on the x axis (or abscissa.)

   a. BDDC   b. BIBO stability
   c. Domain   d. 15 theorem

27. In mathematics, a differential operator is an operator defined as a function of the _____. It is helpful, as a matter of notation first, to consider differentiation as an abstract operation, accepting a function and returning another (in the style of a higher-order function in computer science.)

There are certainly reasons not to restrict to linear operators; for instance the Schwarzian derivative is a well-known non-linear operator.

   a. Vector Laplacian
   b. Second partial derivatives test
   c. Surface integral
   d. Differentiation operator

28. In physics, and more specifically kinematics, _____ is the change in velocity over time. Because velocity is a vector, it can change in two ways: a change in magnitude and/or a change in direction. In one dimension, _____ is the rate at which something speeds up or slows down.
   a. ACTRAN
   b. Acceleration
   c. AUSM
   d. ALGOR

29. Let f be a differentiable function, and let f'(x) be its derivative. The derivative of f'(x) (if it has one) is written f''(x) and is called the _____ of f. Similarly, the derivative of a _____, if it exists, is written f'''(x) and is called the third derivative of f.
   a. Stationary phase approximation
   b. Second derivative
   c. Ramp function
   d. Horizontal asymptote

30. Let f be a differentiable function, and let f'(x) be its derivative. The derivative of f'(x) (if it has one) is written f''(x) and is called the second derivative of f. Similarly, the derivative of a second derivative, if it exists, is written f'''(x) and is called the _____ of f.
   a. Semi-differentiability
   b. Second derivative
   c. Third derivative
   d. Geometric function theory

31. In mathematics and its applications, _____ refers to finding the linear approximation to a function at a given point. In the study of dynamical systems, _____ is a method for assessing the local stability of an equilibrium point of a system of nonlinear differential equations or discrete dynamical systems. This method is used in fields such as engineering, physics, economics, and ecology.
   a. Stationary point
   b. Point of inflection
   c. Symmetrically continuous
   d. Linearization

32. In mathematics, a _____ is an approximation of a general function using a linear function (more precisely, an affine function.)

Given a differentiable function f of one real variable, Taylor's theorem for n=1 states that

$$f(x) = f(a) + f'(a)(x-a) + R_2$$

Chapter 2. Limits and Derivatives

where R₂ is the remainder term. The _____ is obtained by dropping the remainder:

$$f(x) \approx f(a) + f\,'(a)(x-a)$$

which is true for x close to a.

a. Smooth function
c. Linear Approximation
b. Linearity of differentiation
d. Differentiation of trigonometric functions

33. In mathematics, a _____ is a function which preserves the given order. This concept first arose in calculus, and was later generalized to the more abstract setting of order theory.

In calculus, a function f defined on a subset of the real numbers with real values is called monotonic (also monotonically increasing or non-decreasing), if for all x and y such that x >≤ y one has f(x) >≤ f(y), so f preserves the order.

a. Pseudo-differential operator
c. 15 theorem
b. Pettis integral
d. Monotonic function

34. In a totally ordered set all elements are mutually comparable, so such a set can have at most one minimal element and at most one maximal element. Then, due to mutual comparability, the minimal element will also be the least element and the maximal element will also be the greatest element. Thus in a totally ordered set we can simply use the terms minimum and _____.

a. Dirichlet integral
c. Complex analysis
b. Hyperbolic angle
d. Maximum

35. In a totally ordered set all elements are mutually comparable, so such a set can have at most one minimal element and at most one maximal element. Then, due to mutual comparability, the minimal element will also be the least element and the maximal element will also be the greatest element. Thus in a totally ordered set we can simply use the terms _____ and maximum.

a. Calculus controversy
c. Periodic function
b. Minimum
d. Taylor's theorem

36. In calculus, an _____, primitive or indefinite integral of a function f is a function F whose derivative is equal to f, i.e., F >' = f. The process of solving for antiderivatives is antidifferentiation (or indefinite integration.) Antiderivatives are related to definite integrals through the fundamental theorem of calculus: the definite integral of a function over an interval is equal to the difference between the values of an _____ evaluated at the endpoints of the interval.

a. Integrand
c. Indefinite integral
b. Order of integration
d. Antiderivative

37. In differential calculus, an inflection point, or _____ (or inflexion) is a point on a curve at which the curvature changes sign. The curve changes from being concave upwards (positive curvature) to concave downwards (negative curvature), or vice versa. If one imagines driving a vehicle along the curve, it is a point at which the steering-wheel is momentarily 'straight', being turned from left to right or vice versa.

a. Second derivative test
b. Reduced derivative
c. Linearity of differentiation
d. Point of inflection

Chapter 3. Differentiation Rules

1. In mathematics, a _____ is a function whose values do not vary and thus are constant. For example, if we have the function f(x) = 4, then f is constant since f maps any value to 4. More formally, a function f : A → B is a _____ if f(x) = f(y) for all x and y in A.

    a. Constant function
    b. Range
    c. Piecewise-defined function
    d. Surjective

2. In calculus, a branch of mathematics, the _____ is a measurement of how a function changes when its input changes. Loosely speaking, a _____ can be thought of as how much a quantity is changing at some given point. For example, the _____ of the position (or distance) of a vehicle with respect to time is the instantaneous velocity (respectively, instantaneous speed) at which the vehicle is traveling.

    The process of finding a _____ is called differentiation. The fundamental theorem of calculus states that differentiation is the reverse process to integration.

    a. Mountain pass theorem
    b. Concave upwards
    c. Ramp function
    d. Derivative

3. In calculus, the _____ function is zero (A constant function is one that does not depend on the independent variable, such as f(x) = 7.)

    The rule can be justified in various ways. The derivative is the slope of the tangent to the given function's graph, and the graph of a constant function is a horizontal line, whose slope is zero.

    a. Symmetric derivative
    b. Linearity of differentiation
    c. Derivative of a constant
    d. Functional derivative

4. In elementary algebra, a _____ is a polynomial with two terms--the sum of two monomials--often bound by parenthesis or brackets when operated upon. It is the simplest kind of polynomial other than monomials.

    - The _____ $a^2 - b^2$ can be factored as the product of two other binomials:

        $a^2 - b^2 = (a + b)(a - b.)$

        This is a special case of the more general formula: $a^{n+1} - b^{n+1} = (a - b) \sum_{k=0}^{n} a^k b^{n-k}$.

    - The product of a pair of linear binomials (ax + b) and (cx + d) is:

        $(ax + b)(cx + d) = acx^2 + axd + bcx + bd.$

    - A _____ raised to the nth power, represented as

        $(a + b)^n$

        can be expanded by means of the _____ theorem or, equivalently, using Pascal's triangle. Taking a simple example, the perfect square _____ $(p + q)^2$ can be found by squaring the :first digit, adding twice the product of the first and second digit and finally adding the square of the second digit, to give $p^2 + 2pq + q^2$.

a. Multinomial theorem	b. Partial fractions
c. Binomial	d. Completing the square

5. In mathematics, the _____ is an important formula giving the expansion of powers of sums. Its simplest version states that

$$(x+y)^n = \sum_{k=0}^{n} \binom{n}{k} x^{n-k} y^k \qquad (1)$$

for any real or complex numbers x and y, and any non-negative integer n. The binomial coefficient appearing in (1) may be defined in terms of the factorial function n!:

$$\binom{n}{k} = \frac{n!}{k!\,(n-k)!}.$$

For example, here are the cases where 2 ≤ n ≤ 5:

$$(x+y)^2 = x^2 + 2xy + y^2$$
$$(x+y)^3 = x^3 + 3x^2y + 3xy^2 + y^3$$
$$(x+y)^4 = x^4 + 4x^3y + 6x^2y^2 + 4xy^3 + y^4$$
$$(x+y)^5 = x^5 + 5x^4y + 10x^3y^2 + 10x^2y^3 + 5xy^4 + y^5.$$

Formula (1) is valid more generally for any elements x and y of a semiring as long as xy = yx.

a. Stirling transform	b. Lah numbers
c. Trinomial expansion	d. Binomial Theorem

6. This article will state and prove the _____ for differentiation, and then use it to prove these two formulas.

The _____ for differentiation states that for every natural number n, the derivative of $f(x) = x^n$ is $f'(x) = nx^{n-1}$, that is,

$$(x^n)' = nx^{n-1}.$$

The _____ for integration

$$\int x^n \, dx = \frac{x^{n+1}}{n+1} + C$$

for natural n is then an easy consequence. One just needs to take the derivative of this equality and use the _____ and linearity of differentiation on the right-hand side.

a. Dirichlet integral
c. Power Rule
b. Hyperbolic angle
d. Limits of integration

7. In calculus, the _____ allows you to take constants outside a derivative and concentrate on differentiating the function of x itself. This is a part of the linearity of differentiation.

Suppose you have a function

$$g(x) = k \cdot f(x).$$

where k is a constant.

Use the formula for differentiation from first principles to obtain:

$$g'(x) = \lim_{h \to 0} \frac{g(x+h) - g(x)}{h}$$
$$g'(x) = \lim_{h \to 0} \frac{k \cdot f(x+h) - k \cdot f(x)}{h}$$
$$g'(x) = \lim_{h \to 0} \frac{k(f(x+h) - f(x))}{h}$$
$$g'(x) = k \lim_{h \to 0} \frac{f(x+h) - f(x)}{h} \quad (*)$$
$$g'(x) = k \cdot f'(x).$$

This is the statement of the _____, in Lagrange's notation for differentiation.

a. Reciprocal Rule
c. Constant factor rule in differentiation
b. Differentiation rules
d. Product rule

8. The _____ is a function in mathematics. The application of this function to a value x is written as exp(x). Equivalently, this can be written in the form e^x, where e is a mathematical constant, the base of the natural logarithm, which equals approximately 2.718281828, and is also known as Euler's number.

a. Area hyperbolic functions
c. ACTRAN
b. Integral part
d. Exponential function

9. In economics, the _____ functional form of production functions is widely used to represent the relationship of an output to inputs. It was proposed by Knut Wicksell (1851-1926), and tested against statistical evidence by Charles Cobb and Paul Douglas in 1900-1928.

For production, the function is

$$Y = AL^\alpha K^\beta,$$

where:

- Y = total production (the monetary value of all goods produced in a year)
- L = labor input
- K = capital input
- A = total factor productivity
- α and β are the output elasticities of labor and capital, respectively. These values are constants determined by available technology.

Output elasticity measures the responsiveness of output to a change in levels of either labor or capital used in production, ceteris paribus. For example if α = 0.15, a 1% increase in labor would lead to approximately a 0.15% increase in output.

a. 15 theorem
b. BDDC
c. BIBO stability
d. Cobb-Douglas

10. In infinitesimal calculus, a _____ is traditionally an infinitesimally small change in a variable. For example, if x is a variable, then a change in the value of x is often denoted Δx (or δx when this change is considered to be small.) The _____ dx represents such a change, but is infinitely small.

a. Dirichlet integral
b. Differential
c. Related rates
d. Continuous function

11. A _____ is a mathematical equation for an unknown function of one or several variables that relates the values of the function itself and of its derivatives of various orders. they play a prominent role in engineering, physics, economics and other disciplines.

A simplified real world example of a _____ is modeling the acceleration of a ball falling through the air (considering only gravity and air resistance.)

a. Petrovsky lacuna
b. Differential equation
c. Structural stability
d. Lax pair

12. In the two-dimensional case, a _____ perpendicularly intersects the tangent line to a curve at a given point.

The _____ is often used in computer graphics to determine a surface's orientation toward a light source for flat shading, or the orientation of each of the corners (vertices) to mimic a curved surface with Phong shading.

For a polygon (such as a triangle), a surface normal can be calculated as the vector cross product of two (non-parallel) edges of the polygon.

a. Normal line
b. Prolate
c. Parametric surface
d. PDE surfaces

13. In calculus, the _____ is a formula used to find the derivatives of products of functions. It may be stated thus:

$$(f \cdot g)' = f' \cdot g + f \cdot g'$$

or in the Leibniz notation thus:

$$\frac{d}{dx}(u \cdot v) = u \cdot \frac{dv}{dx} + v \cdot \frac{du}{dx}.$$

Discovery of this rule is credited to Gottfried Leibniz, who demonstrated it using differentials. Here is Leibniz's argument: Let u and v be two differentiable functions of x.

a. Quotient Rule
b. Reciprocal Rule
c. Constant factor rule in differentiation
d. Product Rule

14. In calculus, the _____ is a method of finding the derivative of a function that is the quotient of two other functions for which derivatives exist.

If the function one wishes to differentiate, f(x), can be written as

$$f(x) = \frac{g(x)}{h(x)}$$

and h(x) ≠ 0, then the rule states that the derivative of g(x) / h(x) is equal to:

$$\frac{d}{dx}f(x) = f'(x) = \frac{g'(x)h(x) - g(x)h'(x)}{[h(x)]^2}.$$

Or, more precisely, if all x in some open set containing the number a satisfy h(x) ≠ 0; and g'(a) and h'(a) both exist; then, f'(a) exists as well and:

$$f'(a) = \frac{g'(a)h(a) - g(a)h'(a)}{[h(a)]^2}.$$

The derivative of (4x − 2) / (x² + 1) is:

$$\frac{d}{dx}\left[\frac{(4x-2)}{x^2+1}\right] = \frac{(x^2+1)(4)-(4x-2)(2x)}{(x^2+1)^2}$$

$$= \frac{(4x^2+4)-(8x^2-4x)}{(x^2+1)^2} = \frac{-4x^2+4x+4}{(x^2+1)^2}$$

In the example above, the choices

g(x) = 4x − 2
h(x) = x² + 1

were made. Analogously, the derivative of sin(x) / x² (when x ≠ 0) is:

$$\frac{\cos(x)x^2 - \sin(x)2x}{x^4}$$

Another example is:

$$f(x) = \frac{2x^2}{x^3}$$

whereas g(x) = 2x² and h(x) = x³, and g'(x) = 4x and h'(x) = 3x².

a. Differentiation rules
b. Product rule
c. Reciprocal Rule
d. Quotient Rule

15. In mathematics, the _____ , is the curve defined as follows.

Starting with a fixed circle, a point O on the circle is chosen. For any other point A on the circle, the secant line OA is drawn. The point M is diametrically opposite O. The line OA intersects the tangent at M at the point N. The line parallel to OM through N, and the line perpendicular to OM through A intersect at P. As the point A is varied, the path of P is the witch.

a. Cochleoid
b. Closed curve
c. Witch of Agnesi
d. Folium of Descartes

16. In calculus, the _____ is a shorthand method of finding the derivative of a function that is the reciprocal of a differentiable function, without using the quotient rule or chain rule.

Chapter 3. Differentiation Rules

The _____ states that the derivative of 1 / g(x) is given by

$$\frac{d}{dx}\left(\frac{1}{g(x)}\right) = \frac{-g'(x)}{(g(x))^2}$$

where $g(x) \neq 0$.

The _____ is derived from the quotient rule, with the numerator f(x) = 1. Then,

It is also possible to derive the _____ from the chain rule, by a process very much like that of the derivation of the quotient rule.

    a. Constant factor rule in differentiation   b. Differentiation rules
    c. Quotient Rule   d. Reciprocal Rule

17. In physics, _____ is defined as the rate of change of position. it is vector physical quantity; both speed and direction are required to define it. In the SI (metric) system, it is measured in meters per second: (m/s) or ms^{-1}.
    a. BIBO stability   b. BDDC
    c. Velocity   d. 15 theorem

18. The _____ of a material is defined as its mass per unit volume. The symbol of _____ is ρ '>rho.)

Mathematically:

$$d = \frac{m}{V}$$

where:

        d is the _____,
        m is the mass,
        V is the volume.

    a. BDDC   b. BIBO stability
    c. Density   d. 15 theorem

19. _____, linear mass density or linear mass is a measure of mass per unit of length, and it is a characteristic of strings or other one-dimensional objects. The SI unit of _____ is the kilogram per metre (kg/m.) The _____, μ (sometimes denoted by λ), of an object is defined as:

$$\mu = \frac{\partial m}{\partial x}$$

where m is the mass, and x is a coordinate along the (one dimensional) object.

a. BDDC
b. BIBO stability
c. Linear density
d. 15 theorem

20. An _____ process is a change in which the temperature of the system stays constant: ΔT = 0. This typically occurs when a system is in contact with an outside thermal reservoir (heat bath), and the change occurs slowly enough to allow the system to continually adjust to the temperature of the reservoir through heat exchange. An alternative special case in which a system exchanges no heat with its surroundings (Q = 0) is called an adiabatic process.

a. ALGOR
b. AUSM
c. ACTRAN
d. Isothermal

21. In mathematics, the simplest case of _____ refers to the study of problems in which one seeks to minimize or maximize a real function by systematically choosing the values of real or integer variables from within an allowed set. This (a scalar real valued objective function) is actually a small subset of this field which comprises a large area of applied mathematics and generalizes to study of means to obtain 'best available' values of some objective function given a defined domain where the elaboration is on the types of functions and the conditions and nature of the objects in the problem domain.

The first _____ technique, which is known as steepest descent, goes back to Gauss.

a. Optimization
b. AUSM
c. ACTRAN
d. ALGOR

22. Jean Baptiste _____ (March 21, 1768 - May 16, 1830) was a French mathematician and physicist best known for initiating the investigation of Fourier series and their application to problems of heat flow. The Fourier transform is also named in his honour. Fourier is also generally credited with the discovery of the greenhouse effect.

a. Joseph Fourier
b. 15 theorem
c. BIBO stability
d. BDDC

23. A _____ or Gompertz function, named after Benjamin Gompertz, is a sigmoid function. It is a type of mathematical model for a time series, where growth is slowest at the start and end of a time period. Graphs of Gompertz curves, showing the effect of varying one of a,b,c while keeping the others constant.

$$y(t) = ae^{be^{ct}}$$

where

- a is the upper asymptote
- c is the growth rate
- b, c are negative numbers
- e is Euler's Number (e = 2.71828...)

The function curve can be derived from Gompertz's law, which states the rate of mortality (decay) falls exponentially with current size. Mathematically

$$k^r \propto \frac{1}{y(t)}$$

where

- $r = \frac{y'(t)}{y(t)}$ is the rate of growth.
- k is an arbitrary constant.

Examples of uses for Gompertz curves include:

- Mobile phone uptake, where costs were initially high (so uptake was slow), followed by a period of rapid growth, followed by a slowing of uptake as saturation was reached.
- Population in a confined space, as birth rates first increase and then slow as resource limits are reached.
- Modeling of growth of tumors

In the sixties A.K. Laird for the first time successfully used the _____ to fit data of growth of tumors. In fact, tumors are cellular populations growing in a confined space where the availability of nutrients is limited.

a. Spheroidal wave functions
c. Neumann-Dirichlet method
b. Duffing equation
d. Gompertz curve

24. Trigonometry is a branch of mathematics that deals with triangles, particularly those plane triangles in which one angle has 90 degrees (right triangles.) Trigonometry deals with relationships between the sides and the angles of triangles and with the _____ functions, which describe those relationships.

Trigonometry has applications in both pure mathematics and in applied mathematics, where it is essential in many branches of science and technology.

a. Trigonometric
c. 15 theorem
b. Trigonometric integrals
d. Trigonometric functions

Chapter 3. Differentiation Rules

25. In mathematics, the _____ are functions of an angle. They are important in the study of triangles and modeling periodic phenomena, among many other applications. _____ are commonly defined as ratios of two sides of a right triangle containing the angle, and can equivalently be defined as the lengths of various line segments from a unit circle.

   a. Trigonometric
   b. Trigonometric functions
   c. 15 theorem
   d. Trigonometric integrals

26. The _____ are a pair of first order, non-linear, differential equations frequently used to describe the dynamics of biological systems in which two species interact, one a predator and one its prey. They were proposed independently by Alfred J. Lotka in 1925 and Vito Volterra in 1926.

>

>

where

- y is the number of some predator;
- x is the number of its prey;
- dy/dt and dx/dt represents the growth of the two populations against time;
- t represents the time; and
- >α, >β, >γ and >δ are parameters representing the interaction of the two species.

When multiplied out, the equations take a form useful for physical interpretation. Their origin should be considered from a more general framework,

>
>

where both functions represent per capita growth rates of the prey and predator, respectively.

   a. BIBO stability
   b. 15 theorem
   c. BDDC
   d. Lotka-Volterra equations

27. In mathematics, the concept of a '_____' is used to describe the behavior of a function as its argument or input either 'gets close' to some point, or as the argument becomes arbitrarily large; or the behavior of a sequence's elements as their index increases indefinitely. Limits are used in calculus and other branches of mathematical analysis to define derivatives and continuity.

In formulas, _____ is usually abbreviated as lim

a. 15 theorem
b. BIBO stability
c. BDDC
d. Limit

28. _____ is the motion of a simple harmonic oscillator, a motion that is neither driven nor damped. The motion is periodic - as it repeats itself at standard intervals in a specific manner - and sinusoidal, with constant amplitude; the acceleration of a body executing _____ is directly proportional to the displacement of the body from the equilibrium position and is always directed towards the equilibrium position.

The motion is characterized by its amplitude (which is always positive), its period, the time for a single oscillation, its frequency, the reciprocal of the period (i.e. the number of cycles per unit time), and its phase, which determines the starting point on the sine wave.

a. 15 theorem
b. Holonomic
c. BDDC
d. Simple harmonic motion

29. In acoustics and telecommunication, a _____ of a wave is a component frequency of the signal that is an integer multiple of the fundamental frequency. For example, if the fundamental frequency is f, the harmonics have frequencies f, 2f, 3f, 4f, etc. The harmonics have the property that they are all periodic at the fundamental frequency, therefore the sum of harmonics is also periodic at that frequency.

a. Harmonic
b. 15 theorem
c. BIBO stability
d. BDDC

30. In mathematics, a _____ is a constant multiplicative factor of a certain object. For example, in the expression $9x^2$, the _____ of x^2 is 9.

The object can be such things as a variable, a vector, a function, etc.

a. Leading coefficient
b. Difference polynomial
c. Coefficient
d. Degree of the polynomial

31. In mathematics, a _____ represents the application of one function to the results of another. For instance, the functions f: X → Y and g: Y → Z can be composed by first computing f(x) and then applying a function g to the output of f(x.)

Thus one obtains a function g ∘ f: X → Z defined by (g ∘ f)(x) = g(f(x)) for all x in X. The notation g ∘ f is read as 'g circle f', or 'g composed with f', 'g after f', 'g following f', or just 'g of f'.

a. Composite function
b. Range
c. Surjective
d. Constant function

32. In mathematics, _____ are a method of defining a curve. A simple kinematical example is when one uses a time parameter to determine the position, velocity, and other information about a body in motion.

Abstractly, a relation is given in the form of an equation, and it is shown also to be the image of functions from items such as R^n.

a. Laplace operator
b. Parametric equations
c. Multivariable calculus
d. Differential operator

33. In geometry, the _____ (or simply the tangent) to a curve at a given point is the straight line that 'just touches' the curve at that point (in the sense explained more precisely below.) As it passes through the point of tangency, the _____ is 'going in the same direction' as the curve, and in this sense it is the best straight-line approximation to the curve at that point. The same definition applies to space curves and curves in n-dimensional Euclidean space.

a. Sphere
b. Lie derivative
c. Minimal surface
d. Tangent line

34. In mathematics, a (topological) _____ is defined as follows: let I be an interval of real numbers (i.e. a non-empty connected subset of $\mathbb{R}$); then a _____ γ is a continuous mapping $\gamma : I \to X$, where X is a topological space. The _____ γ is said to be simple if it is injective, i.e. if for all x, y in I, we have $\gamma(x) = \gamma(y) \implies x = y$. If I is a closed bounded interval $[a, b]$, we also allow the possibility $\gamma(a) = \gamma(b)$ (this convention makes it possible to talk about closed simple _____.)

a. Tractrix
b. Prolate cycloid
c. Closed curve
d. Curve

35. In mathematics, a _____ is a unicursal quartic curve with three inflection points, given by the equation

$$a^2 y^2 - b^2 x^2 = x^2 y^2$$

The bullet curve has three double points in the real projective plane, at x=0 and y=0, x=0 and z=0, and y=0 and z=0, and is therefore a unicursal (rational) curve of genus zero.

If

$$f(z) = \sum_{n=0}^{\infty} \binom{2n}{n} z^{2n+1} = z + 2z^3 + 6z^5 + 20z^7 + \cdots$$

then

$$y = f\left(\frac{x}{2a}\right) \pm 2b$$

are the two branches of the bullet curve at the origin.

a. Folium of Descartes
b. Closed curve
c. Hypocycloid
d. Bullet-nose curve

Chapter 3. Differentiation Rules

36. In the mathematical field of numerical analysis, a _____ is a parametric curve important in computer graphics and related fields. Generalizations of Bezier curves to higher dimensions are called Bezier surfaces, of which the Bezier triangle is a special case.

Bezier curves were widely publicized in 1962 by the French engineer Pierre B>ézier, who used them to design automobile bodies.

- a. BIBO stability
- b. BDDC
- c. 15 theorem
- d. Bezier curve

37. In calculus, a method called _____ can be applied to implicitly defined functions. This method is an application of the chain rule allowing one to calculate the derivative of a function given implicitly.

As explained in the introduction, y can be given as a function of x implicitly rather than explicitly. When we have an equation R (x,y) = 0, we may be able to solve it for y and then differentiate. However, sometimes it is simpler to differentiate R(x,y) with respect to x and then solve for dy / dx.

- a. Ordinary differential equation
- b. Automatic differentiation
- c. Implicit differentiation
- d. Implicit function

38. In Geometry, the _____ is an algebraic curve defined by the equation

$$x^3 + y^3 - 3axy = 0$$

It forms a loop in the first quadrant with a double point at the origin and asymptote

$$x + y + a = 0$$

It is symmetrical about y = x.

- a. Prolate cycloid
- b. Cochleoid
- c. Curve
- d. Folium of Descartes

39. In mathematics, an _____ is a generalization for the concept of a function in which the dependent variable has not been given 'explicitly' in terms of the independent variable. To give a function f explicitly is to provide a prescription for determining the output value of the function y in terms of the input value x:

y = f(x.)

By contrast, the function is implicit if the value of y is obtained from x by solving an equation of the form:

R(x,y) = 0.

Chapter 3. Differentiation Rules

    a. Implicit function
    b. Implicit differentiation
    c. Automatic differentiation
    d. Ordinary differential equation

40. A surface normal to a flat surface is a vector which is perpendicular to that surface. A normal to a non-flat surface at a point P on the surface is a vector perpendicular to the tangent plane to that surface at P. The word 'normal' is also used as an adjective: a line normal to a plane, the normal component of a force, the _____, etc. The concept of normality generalizes to orthogonality.
    a. Normal vector
    b. Hyperbolic paraboloid
    c. PDE surfaces
    d. Paraboloid

41. In mathematics, two vectors are _____ if they are perpendicular, i.e., they form a right angle. For example, a subway and the street above, although they do not physically intersect, are _____ if they cross at a right angle.
    a. Orthogonal
    b. ALGOR
    c. ACTRAN
    d. AUSM

42. In mathematics, _____ are a family of curves in the plane that intersect a given family of curves at right angles. The problem is classical, but is now understood by means of complex analysis; see for example harmonic conjugate.

For a family of level curves described by g(x,y) = C, where C is a constant, the _____ may be found as the level curves of a new function f(x,y) by solving the partial differential equation

$$\nabla f \cdot \nabla g = 0$$

for f(x,y).

    a. AUSM
    b. ALGOR
    c. Orthogonal trajectories
    d. ACTRAN

43. A _____ is the path a moving object follows through space. The object might be a projectile or a satellite, for example. It thus includes the meaning of orbit - the path of a planet, an asteroid or a comet as it travels around a central mass.
    a. BDDC
    b. 15 theorem
    c. BIBO stability
    d. Trajectory

44. In mathematics, a _____ is the graph of the system of parametric equations

$$x = A\sin(at + \delta), \quad y = B\sin(bt),$$

which describes complex harmonic motion. This family of curves was investigated by Nathaniel Bowditch in 1815, and later in more detail by Jules Antoine Lissajous in 1857.

The appearance of the figure is highly sensitive to the ratio a/b.

a. BDDC
b. 15 theorem
c. BIBO stability
d. Lissajous curve

45. In mathematics, the _____ of a function y = f(x) is a function that, in some fashion, 'undoes' the effect of f The _____ of f is denoted f $^{-1}$. The statements y=f(x) and x=f $^{-1}$(y) are equivalent.
    a. AUSM
    b. ALGOR
    c. Inverse
    d. ACTRAN

46. In mathematics, the _____ or cyclometric functions are the inverse functions of the trigonometric functions. The principal inverses are listed in the following table.

If x is allowed to be a complex number, then the range of y applies only to its real part.

    a. ALGOR
    b. Inverse trigonometric functions
    c. AUSM
    d. ACTRAN

47. In mathematics, an _____ is a particular type of curve: a hypocycloid with four cusps. Astroids are also superellipses: all astroids are scaled versions of the curve specified by the equation

$$x^{2/3} + y^{2/3} = 1.$$

Its modern name comes from the Greek word for 'star'.

    a. ACTRAN
    b. Epicycloid
    c. Astroid
    d. ALGOR

48. The _____ is a curve, with a Cartesian equation of

$$x^4 = x^2 + y^2,$$

or, in polar coordinates,

$$r = \sec^2 \theta.$$

This quartic curve was studied by the Greek astronomer and mathematician Eudoxus of Cnidus (c. 408 BC - c.347 BC) in relation to the classical problem of doubling the cube.

- List of curves

.

    a. Kampyle of Eudoxus
    b. Macbeath surface
    c. Tschirnhausen cubic
    d. Dolbeault operator

Chapter 3. Differentiation Rules

49. In a totally ordered set all elements are mutually comparable, so such a set can have at most one minimal element and at most one maximal element. Then, due to mutual comparability, the minimal element will also be the least element and the maximal element will also be the greatest element. Thus in a totally ordered set we can simply use the terms minimum and _____.

    a. Complex analysis   b. Dirichlet integral
    c. Hyperbolic angle   d. Maximum

50. In a totally ordered set all elements are mutually comparable, so such a set can have at most one minimal element and at most one maximal element. Then, due to mutual comparability, the minimal element will also be the least element and the maximal element will also be the greatest element. Thus in a totally ordered set we can simply use the terms _____ and maximum.

    a. Taylor's theorem   b. Calculus controversy
    c. Periodic function   d. Minimum

51. In mathematics, _____, first defined by the mathematician Daniel Bernoulli and generalized by Friedrich Bessel, are canonical solutions y(x) of Bessel's differential equation:

$$x^2 \frac{d^2 y}{dx^2} + x \frac{dy}{dx} + (x^2 - \alpha^2)y = 0$$

for an arbitrary real or complex number α (the order of the Bessel function.) The most common and important special case is where α is an integer n.

Although α and −α produce the same differential equation, it is conventional to define different _____ for these two orders (e.g., so that the _____ are mostly smooth functions of α.)

    a. 15 theorem   b. Bessel functions
    c. Multiplication theorem   d. Logarithmic integral function

52. In mathematics, if f is a function from A to B then an _____ for f is a function in the opposite direction, from B to A, with the property that a round trip (a composition) from A to B to A (or from B to A to B) returns each element of the initial set to itself. Thus, if an input x into the function f produces an output y, then inputting y into the _____ f^{-1} (read f inverse, not to be confused with exponentiation) produces the output x. Not every function has an inverse; those that do are called invertible.

    a. Augustin-Jean Fresnel   b. Augustin Louis Cauchy
    c. Aristotle   d. Inverse function

53. The function $\log_b(x)$ depends on both b and x, but the term _____ in standard usage refers to a function of the form $\log_b(x)$ in which the base b is fixed and so the only argument is x. Thus there is one _____ for each value of the base b (which must be positive and must differ from 1.) Viewed in this way, the base-b _____ is the inverse function of the exponential function b^x.

    a. 15 theorem   b. BIBO stability
    c. BDDC   d. Logarithm function

54. In mathematics, specifically in calculus and complex analysis, the _____ of a function f is defined by the formula

Chapter 3. Differentiation Rules

$$\frac{f'}{f}$$

where f ' is the derivative of f.

When f is a function f(x) of a real variable x, and takes real, strictly positive values, this is indeed the formula for (log f)', that is, the derivative of the natural logarithm of f, as follows directly from the chain rule.

Many properties of the real logarithm also apply to the _____, even when the function does not take values in the positive reals.

- a. Difference quotient
- b. Symmetric derivative
- c. Linearity of differentiation
- d. Logarithmic derivative

55. Integration is an important concept in mathematics, specifically in the field of calculus and, more broadly, mathematical analysis. Given a function f of a real variable x and an interval [a, b] of the real line, the _____

$$\int_a^b f(x)\,dx\,,$$

is defined informally to be the net signed area of the region in the xy-plane bounded by the graph of f, the x-axis, and the vertical lines x = a and x = b.

The term '_____' may also refer to the notion of antiderivative, a function F whose derivative is the given function f.

- a. Integral test for convergence
- b. Integral
- c. Indefinite integral
- d. Integrand

56. In physics and geometry, the _____ is the theoretical shape of a hanging flexible chain or cable when supported at its ends and acted upon by a uniform gravitational force (its own weight) and in equilibrium. The curve has a U shape that is similar in appearance to the parabola, though it is a different curve.
- a. BDDC
- b. 15 theorem
- c. BIBO stability
- d. Catenary

57. In mathematics, the _____ are analogs of the ordinary trigonometric or circular functions. The basic _____ are the hyperbolic sine 'sinh', and the hyperbolic cosine 'cosh', from which are derived the hyperbolic tangent 'tanh', etc., in analogy to the derived trigonometric functions. The inverse _____ are the area hyperbolic sine 'arsinh' (also called 'asinh', or sometimes by the misnomer of 'arcsinh') and so on.
- a. Step function
- b. Hyperbolic sine
- c. Hyperbolic tangent
- d. Hyperbolic functions

Chapter 3. Differentiation Rules

58. In mathematics, a _____ is an approximation of a general function using a linear function (more precisely, an affine function.)

Given a differentiable function f of one real variable, Taylor's theorem for n=1 states that

$$f(x) = f(a) + f'(a)(x-a) + R_2$$

where R_2 is the remainder term. The _____ is obtained by dropping the remainder:

$$f(x) \approx f(a) + f'(a)(x-a)$$

which is true for x close to a.

    a. Linearity of differentiation   b. Differentiation of trigonometric functions
    c. Linear approximation   d. Smooth function

59. In mathematics and its applications, _____ refers to finding the linear approximation to a function at a given point. In the study of dynamical systems, _____ is a method for assessing the local stability of an equilibrium point of a system of nonlinear differential equations or discrete dynamical systems. This method is used in fields such as engineering, physics, economics, and ecology.

    a. Point of inflection   b. Symmetrically continuous
    c. Stationary point   d. Linearization

60. In mathematics and physics, the _____ or Laplacian, denoted by Δ or ∇^2 and named after Pierre-Simon de Laplace, is a differential operator, specifically an important case of an elliptic operator, with many applications. In physics, it is used in modeling of wave propagation, heat flow and forming the Helmholtz equation. It is central in electrostatics and fluid mechanics, anchoring in Laplace's equation and Poisson's equation.

    a. Partial derivative   b. Vector Laplacian
    c. Laplace operator   d. Differentiation operator

61. One commonly distinguishes between the _____ and the absolute error. The absolute error is the magnitude of the difference between the exact value and the approximation. The _____ is the absolute error divided by the magnitude of the exact value.

    a. Relative error   b. Meshfree methods
    c. Numerical integration   d. Series acceleration

62. The _____ in some data is the discrepancy between an exact value and some approximation to it. An _____ can occur because

1. the measurement of the data is not precise (due to the instruments), or
2. approximations are used instead of the real data (e.g., 3.14 instead of π.)

In the mathematical field of numerical analysis, the numerical stability of an algorithm in numerical analysis indicates how the error is propagated by the algorithm.

One commonly distinguishes between the relative error and the absolute error. The absolute error is the magnitude of the difference between the exact value and the approximation.

   a. AUSM
   b. ALGOR
   c. Approximation error
   d. ACTRAN

63. In calculus, _____ gives a sequence of approximations of a differentiable function around a given point by polynomials (the Taylor polynomials of that function) whose coefficients depend only on the derivatives of the function at that point. The theorem also gives precise estimates on the size of the error in the approximation. The theorem is named after the mathematician Brook Taylor, who stated it in 1712, though the result was first discovered 41 years earlier in 1671 by James Gregory.

   a. Complex analysis
   b. Leibniz differential
   c. Taylor's theorem
   d. Continuous function

64. In mathematics, an _____ is an infinite series of the form

$$\sum_{n=0}^{\infty} (-1)^n a_n,$$

with $a_n \geq 0$ (or $a_n \leq 0$) for all n. A finite sum of this kind is an alternating sum. An _____ converges if the terms a_n converge to 0 monotonically.

   a. Uniform convergence
   b. Alternating Series
   c. Extreme value
   d. Infinite series

65. In mathematics, a _____ (or just conic) is a curve obtained by intersecting a cone (more precisely, a circular conical surface) with a plane. A _____ is therefore a restriction of a quadric surface to the plane. The conic sections were named and studied as long ago as 200 BC, when Apollonius of Perga undertook a systematic study of their properties.

   a. Foci
   b. 15 theorem
   c. BDDC
   d. Conic section

Chapter 4. Applications of Differentiation

1. In differential calculus, _____ problems involve finding a rate that a quantity changes by relating the population of the earth. The rate of change is usually with respect to people who have died.

   a. Related rates
   b. Binomial series
   c. Reflection formula
   d. Complex analysis

2. In mathematics, the simplest case of _____ refers to the study of problems in which one seeks to minimize or maximize a real function by systematically choosing the values of real or integer variables from within an allowed set. This (a scalar real valued objective function) is actually a small subset of this field which comprises a large area of applied mathematics and generalizes to study of means to obtain 'best available' values of some objective function given a defined domain where the elaboration is on the types of functions and the conditions and nature of the objects in the problem domain.

   The first _____ technique, which is known as steepest descent, goes back to Gauss.

   a. ACTRAN
   b. ALGOR
   c. Optimization
   d. AUSM

3. In economics, the _____ functional form of production functions is widely used to represent the relationship of an output to inputs. It was proposed by Knut Wicksell (1851-1926), and tested against statistical evidence by Charles Cobb and Paul Douglas in 1900-1928.

   For production, the function is

   $$Y = AL^{\alpha}K^{\beta},$$

   where:

   - Y = total production (the monetary value of all goods produced in a year)
   - L = labor input
   - K = capital input
   - A = total factor productivity
   - α and β are the output elasticities of labor and capital, respectively. These values are constants determined by available technology.

   Output elasticity measures the responsiveness of output to a change in levels of either labor or capital used in production, ceteris paribus. For example if α = 0.15, a 1% increase in labor would lead to approximately a 0.15% increase in output.

   a. BDDC
   b. 15 theorem
   c. BIBO stability
   d. Cobb-Douglas

4. The largest and the smallest element of a set are called extreme values, absolute extrema, or extreme records.

For a differentiable function f, if f(x_0) is an _____ for the set of all values f(x), and if x_0 is in the interior of the domain of f, then x_0 is a critical point, by Fermat's theorem.

In the case of a general partial order one should not confuse a least element (smaller than all other) and a minimal element (nothing is smaller.)

    a. Integration by substitution
    b. Extreme Value Theorem
    c. Infinitesimal
    d. Extreme value

5. In a totally ordered set all elements are mutually comparable, so such a set can have at most one minimal element and at most one maximal element. Then, due to mutual comparability, the minimal element will also be the least element and the maximal element will also be the greatest element. Thus in a totally ordered set we can simply use the terms minimum and _____.

    a. Maximum
    b. Complex analysis
    c. Dirichlet integral
    d. Hyperbolic angle

6. In a totally ordered set all elements are mutually comparable, so such a set can have at most one minimal element and at most one maximal element. Then, due to mutual comparability, the minimal element will also be the least element and the maximal element will also be the greatest element. Thus in a totally ordered set we can simply use the terms _____ and maximum.

    a. Calculus controversy
    b. Periodic function
    c. Taylor's theorem
    d. Minimum

7. In mathematics, the concept of a '_____' is used to describe the behavior of a function as its argument or input either 'gets close' to some point, or as the argument becomes arbitrarily large; or the behavior of a sequence's elements as their index increases indefinitely. Limits are used in calculus and other branches of mathematical analysis to define derivatives and continuity.

In formulas, _____ is usually abbreviated as lim

    a. BIBO stability
    b. 15 theorem
    c. BDDC
    d. Limit

8. In calculus, the _____ states that if a real-valued function f is continuous in the closed and bounded interval [a,b], then f must attain its maximum and minimum value, each at least once. That is, there exist numbers c and d in [a,b] such that:

$$f(c) \geq f(x) \geq f(d) \quad \text{for all } x \in [a, b].$$

A related theorem is the boundedness theorem which states that a continuous function f in the closed interval [a,b] is bounded on that interval. That is, there exist real numbers m and M such that:

$$m \leq f(x) \leq M \quad \text{for all } x \in [a, b].$$

The _____ enriches the boundedness theorem by saying that not only is the function bounded, but it also attains its least upper bound as its maximum and its greatest lower bound as its minimum.

- a. Integral of secant cubed
- b. Infinitesimal
- c. Uniform convergence
- d. Extreme Value Theorem

9. In mathematics, a _____ (or critical number) is a point on the domain of a function where:

- one dimension: the derivative (or slope of the line when visualized) is equal to zero or a point where the function ceases to be differentiable.
- in general: there are two distinct concepts: either the derivative (Jacobian) vanishes, or it is not of full rank (or, in either case, the function is not differentiable); these agree in one dimension.

Note that in one dimension, a critical value or critical number x of function f is the domain element at which the derivative is zero or undefined, whereas the associated ordered pair (x, y) is the _____. In higher dimensions a critical value is in the range whereas a _____ is in the domain.

There are two situations in which a point becomes a _____ of a function of one variable. The first of which is that the value of the first derivative is equal to zero.

- a. Shift theorem
- b. Differential operator
- c. Differentiation operator
- d. Critical point

10. In mathematics, a _____ is a constant multiplicative factor of a certain object. For example, in the expression $9x^2$, the _____ of x^2 is 9.

The object can be such things as a variable, a vector, a function, etc.

- a. Degree of the polynomial
- b. Leading coefficient
- c. Difference polynomial
- d. Coefficient

11. In probability theory and statistics, the _____ (or expectation value or mean and for continuous random variables with a density function it is the probability density -weighted integral of the possible values.

The term '_____' can be misleading.

- a. ACTRAN
- b. ALGOR
- c. AUSM
- d. Expected value

Chapter 4. Applications of Differentiation

12. In calculus, the _____ states, roughly, that given a section of a smooth curve, there is at least one point on that section at which the derivative (slope) of the curve is equal (parallel) to the 'average' derivative of the section. It is used to prove theorems that make global conclusions about a function on an interval starting from local hypotheses about derivatives at points of the interval.

This theorem can be understood concretely by applying it to motion: If a car travels one hundred miles in one hour, so its average speed during that time was 100 miles per hour.

    a. Mean Value Theorem   b. First derivative test
    c. Fresnel integrals   d. Leibniz differential

13. In mathematics, a _____ is a function which preserves the given order. This concept first arose in calculus, and was later generalized to the more abstract setting of order theory.

In calculus, a function f defined on a subset of the real numbers with real values is called monotonic (also monotonically increasing or non-decreasing), if for all x and y such that x >≤ y one has f(x) >≤ f(y), so f preserves the order.

    a. Pseudo-differential operator   b. Pettis integral
    c. 15 theorem   d. Monotonic function

14. In calculus, a branch of mathematics, the _____ is a measurement of how a function changes when its input changes. Loosely speaking, a _____ can be thought of as how much a quantity is changing at some given point. For example, the _____ of the position (or distance) of a vehicle with respect to time is the instantaneous velocity (respectively, instantaneous speed) at which the vehicle is traveling.

The process of finding a _____ is called differentiation. The fundamental theorem of calculus states that differentiation is the reverse process to integration.

    a. Ramp function   b. Concave upwards
    c. Derivative   d. Mountain pass theorem

15. In calculus, the _____ determines whether a given critical point of a function is a maximum, a minimum, or neither.

Suppose that f is a function and we want to determine if f has a maximum or minimum at x. If f is increasing to the left of x and decreasing to the right of x, then x is a local maximum of f.

    a. Test for Divergence   b. First Derivative Test
    c. Functional integration   d. Hyperbolic angle

16. In differential calculus, an inflection point, or _____ (or inflexion) is a point on a curve at which the curvature changes sign. The curve changes from being concave upwards (positive curvature) to concave downwards (negative curvature), or vice versa. If one imagines driving a vehicle along the curve, it is a point at which the steering-wheel is momentarily 'straight', being turned from left to right or vice versa.

a. Second derivative test	b. Reduced derivative
c. Linearity of differentiation	d. Point of inflection

17. Let f be a differentiable function, and let f'(x) be its derivative. The derivative of f'(x) (if it has one) is written f''(x) and is called the _____ of f. Similarly, the derivative of a _____, if it exists, is written f'''(x) and is called the third derivative of f.

a. Second Derivative	b. Stationary phase approximation
c. Horizontal asymptote	d. Ramp function

18. In calculus, a branch of mathematics, the _____ is a criterion often useful for determining whether a given stationary point of a function is a local maximum or a local minimum.

The test states: If the function f is twice differentiable at a stationary point x, meaning that $f'(x) = 0$, then:

- If $f''(x) < 0$ then f has a local maximum at x.
- If $f''(x) > 0$ then f has a local minimum at x.
- If $f''(x) = 0$, the _____ says nothing about the point x, has a possible inflection point.

In the last case, the function may have a local maximum or minimum there, but the function is sufficiently 'flat' that this is undetected by the second derivative. In this case one has to examine the third derivative. Such an example is f(x) = x⁴.

a. Stationary point	b. Parametric derivative
c. Second Derivative Test	d. Metric derivative

19. In geometry, an _____ is a plane curve produced by tracing the path of a chosen point of a circle -- called epicycle -- which rolls without slipping around a fixed circle. It is a particular kind of roulette.

If the smaller circle has radius r, and the larger circle has radius R = kr, then the parametric equations for the curve can be given by either:

$$x(\theta) = (R+r)\cos\theta - r\cos\left(\frac{R+r}{r}\theta\right)$$
$$y(\theta) = (R+r)\sin\theta - r\sin\left(\frac{R+r}{r}\theta\right),$$

or:

$$x(\theta) = r(k+1)\cos\theta - r\cos((k+1)\theta)$$
$$y(\theta) = r(k+1)\sin\theta - r\sin((k+1)\theta).$$

If k is an integer, then the curve is closed, and has k cusps (i.e., sharp corners, where the curve is not differentiable.)

a. Asymptotic curve
b. ACTRAN
c. Epicycloid
d. ALGOR

20. In geometry, a _____ is a special plane curve generated by the trace of a fixed point on a small circle that rolls within a larger circle. It is comparable to the cycloid but instead of the circle rolling along a line, it rolls within a circle. The red curve is a _____ traced as the smaller black circle rolls around inside the larger blue circle (parameters are R=3.0, r=1.0, and so k=3), giving a deltoid.

If the smaller circle has radius r, and the larger circle has radius R = kr, then the parametric equations for the curve can be given by either:

$$x(\theta) = (R - r)\cos\theta + r\cos\left(\frac{R-r}{r}\theta\right)$$
$$y(\theta) = (R - r)\sin\theta - r\sin\left(\frac{R-r}{r}\theta\right),$$

or:

$$x(\theta) = r(k - 1)\cos\theta + r\cos((k - 1)\theta)$$
$$y(\theta) = r(k - 1)\sin\theta - r\sin((k - 1)\theta).$$

If k is an integer, then the curve is closed, and has k cusps (i.e., sharp corners, where the curve is not differentiable.)

a. Kappa curve
b. Closed curve
c. Hypocycloid
d. Bullet-nose curve

21. In calculus and other branches of mathematical analysis, an _____ is an algebraic expression obtained in the context of limits. Limits involving algebraic operations are often performed by replacing subexpressions by their limits; if the expression obtained after this substitution does not give enough information to determine the original limit, it is known as an _____. The indeterminate forms include 0^0, 0/0, 1^∞, $\infty - \infty$, ∞/∞, $0\times\infty$, and ∞^0.

a. ACTRAN
b. AUSM
c. ALGOR
d. Indeterminate form

22. In mathematics, the _____ of a function y = f(x) is a function that, in some fashion, 'undoes' the effect of f The _____ of f is denoted f^{-1}. The statements y=f(x) and x=f^{-1}(y) are equivalent.

a. ACTRAN
b. ALGOR
c. Inverse
d. AUSM

Chapter 4. Applications of Differentiation

23. _____ is the concept of adding accumulated interest back to the principal, so that interest is earned on interest from that moment on. The act of declaring interest to be principal is called compounding (i.e., interest is compounded.) A loan, for example, may have its interest compounded every month: in this case, a loan with $100 principal and 1% interest per month would have a balance of $101 at the end of the first month.
    a. BDDC
    b. 15 theorem
    c. BIBO stability
    d. Compound interest

24. In mathematics, a _____ is the graph of the system of parametric equations

$$x = A\sin(at + \delta), \quad y = B\sin(bt),$$

which describes complex harmonic motion. This family of curves was investigated by Nathaniel Bowditch in 1815, and later in more detail by Jules Antoine Lissajous in 1857.

The appearance of the figure is highly sensitive to the ratio a/b.

    a. Lissajous curve
    b. 15 theorem
    c. BIBO stability
    d. BDDC

25. In mathematics, a _____ (or direction field) is a graphical representation of the solutions of a first-order differential equation. It is achieved without solving the differential equation analytically, and thence it is useful. The representation may be used to qualitatively visualise solutions, or to numerically approximate them.
    a. The Method of Mechanical Theorems
    b. Standard part function
    c. Fresnel integrals
    d. Slope field

26. In infinitesimal calculus, a _____ is traditionally an infinitesimally small change in a variable. For example, if x is a variable, then a change in the value of x is often denoted Δx (or δx when this change is considered to be small.) The _____ dx represents such a change, but is infinitely small.
    a. Differential
    b. Continuous function
    c. Dirichlet integral
    d. Related rates

27. The _____ , are the five positions in an orbital configuration where a small object affected only by gravity can theoretically be stationary relative to two larger objects (such as a satellite with respect to the Earth and Moon.) The _____ mark positions where the combined gravitational pull of the two large masses provides precisely the centripetal force required to rotate with them. They are analogous to geostationary orbits in that they allow an object to be in a 'fixed' position in space rather than an orbit in which its relative position changes continuously.
    a. 15 theorem
    b. BDDC
    c. BIBO stability
    d. Lagrangian points

28. In calculus, an _____, primitive or indefinite integral of a function f is a function F whose derivative is equal to f, i.e., F >' = f. The process of solving for antiderivatives is antidifferentiation (or indefinite integration.) Antiderivatives are related to definite integrals through the fundamental theorem of calculus: the definite integral of a function over an interval is equal to the difference between the values of an _____ evaluated at the endpoints of the interval.
    a. Integrand
    b. Antiderivative
    c. Indefinite integral
    d. Order of integration

29. A _____ is a mathematical equation for an unknown function of one or several variables that relates the values of the function itself and of its derivatives of various orders. they play a prominent role in engineering, physics, economics and other disciplines.

A simplified real world example of a _____ is modeling the acceleration of a ball falling through the air (considering only gravity and air resistance.)

  a. Differential equation   b. Structural stability
  c. Petrovsky lacuna   d. Lax pair

Chapter 5. Integrals

1. In mathematics, a (topological) _____ is defined as follows: let I be an interval of real numbers (i.e. a non-empty connected subset of $\mathbb{R}$); then a _____ γ is a continuous mapping $\gamma : I \to X$, where X is a topological space. The _____ γ is said to be simple if it is injective, i.e. if for all x, y in I, we have $\gamma(x) = \gamma(y) \implies x = y$. If I is a closed bounded interval $[a, b]$, we also allow the possibility $\gamma(a) = \gamma(b)$ (this convention makes it possible to talk about closed simple _____ .)

   a. Curve
   b. Closed curve
   c. Tractrix
   d. Prolate cycloid

2. _____ is the addition of a set of numbers; the result is their sum or total. An interim or present total of a _____ process is termed the running total. The 'numbers' to be summed may be natural numbers, complex numbers, matrices, or still more complicated objects.

   a. Summation
   b. BDDC
   c. BIBO stability
   d. 15 theorem

3. Integration is an important concept in mathematics, specifically in the field of calculus and, more broadly, mathematical analysis. Given a function f of a real variable x and an interval [a, b] of the real line, the _____

$$\int_a^b f(x)\,dx,$$

is defined informally to be the net signed area of the region in the xy-plane bounded by the graph of f, the x-axis, and the vertical lines x = a and x = b.

The term '_____' may also refer to the notion of antiderivative, a function F whose derivative is the given function f.

   a. Integrand
   b. Indefinite integral
   c. Integral test for convergence
   d. Integral

4. In mathematics, a _____ is a series with a constant ratio between successive terms. For example, the series

$$\frac{1}{2} + \frac{1}{4} + \frac{1}{8} + \frac{1}{16} + \cdots$$

is geometric, because each term is equal to half of the previous term. The sum of this series is 1, as illustrated in the following picture:

_____ are one of the simplest examples of infinite series with finite sums.

   a. Sequence transformation
   b. Converge absolutely
   c. Telescoping series
   d. Geometric series

5. If a function has an integral, it is said to be integrable. The function for which the integral is calculated is called the _____. The region over which a function is being integrated is called the domain of integration.

Chapter 5. Integrals

a. Integration by parts
b. Integrand
c. Order of integration
d. Integral test for convergence

6. Continuous functions are of utmost importance in mathematics and applications. However, not all functions are continuous. If a function is not continuous at a point in its domain, one says that it has a _____ there. The set of all points of _____ of a function may be a discrete set, a dense set, or even the entire domain of the function.

a. BDDC
b. Discontinuity
c. 15 theorem
d. BIBO stability

7. In statistics, given a (random) sample $(Y_i, X_{i1}, \ldots, X_{ip})$, $i = 1, \ldots, n$ the most general form of _____ is formulated as

$$Y_i = \beta_0 + \beta_1 \phi_1(X_{i1}) + \ldots + \beta_p \phi_p(X_{ip}) + \varepsilon_i \qquad i = 1, \ldots, n$$

where $\phi_1, \ldots, \phi_p$ may be nonlinear functions.

In matrix notation this model can be written as

$$Y = X\beta + \varepsilon$$

where Y is an n × 1 column vector, X is an n × (p + 1) matrix, β is a (p + 1) × 1 vector of (unobservable) parameters, and ε is an n × 1 vector of errors, which are uncorrelated random variables each with expected value 0 and variance σ^2. Note that depending on the context the sample can be seen as fixed (observable), or random.

a. 15 theorem
b. BDDC
c. BIBO stability
d. Linear model

8. In mathematics, the concept of a '_____' is used to describe the behavior of a function as its argument or input either 'gets close' to some point, or as the argument becomes arbitrarily large; or the behavior of a sequence's elements as their index increases indefinitely. Limits are used in calculus and other branches of mathematical analysis to define derivatives and continuity.

In formulas, _____ is usually abbreviated as lim

a. 15 theorem
b. BDDC
c. BIBO stability
d. Limit

9. In mathematics, a _____ is a method for approximating the total area underneath a curve on a graph, otherwise known as an integral. It may also be used to define the integration operation.

Consider a function $f: D \to \mathbf{R}$, where D is a subset of the real numbers $\mathbf{R}$, and let $I = [a, b]$ be a closed interval contained in D. A finite set of points $\{x_0, x_1, x_2, ... x_n\}$ such that $a = x_0 < x_1 < x_2 ... < x_n = b$ creates a partition

$P = \{[x_0, x_1), [x_1, x_2), ... [x_{n-1}, x_n]\}$

of I.

    a. Riemann sum
    c. Disk integration
    b. Signed measure
    d. Surface of revolution

10.   In infinitesimal calculus, a _____ is traditionally an infinitesimally small change in a variable. For example, if x is a variable, then a change in the value of x is often denoted Δx (or δx when this change is considered to be small.) The _____ dx represents such a change, but is infinitely small.

    a. Related rates
    c. Continuous function
    b. Dirichlet integral
    d. Differential

11.   In mathematics, the _____ are analogs of the ordinary trigonometric or circular functions. The basic _____ are the hyperbolic sine 'sinh', and the hyperbolic cosine 'cosh', from which are derived the hyperbolic tangent 'tanh', etc., in analogy to the derived trigonometric functions. The inverse _____ are the area hyperbolic sine 'arsinh' (also called 'asinh', or sometimes by the misnomer of 'arcsinh') and so on.

    a. Step function
    c. Hyperbolic tangent
    b. Hyperbolic sine
    d. Hyperbolic functions

12.   A _____ is an algebraic equation in which each term is either a constant or the product of a constant and (the first power of) a single variable. Linear equations can have one, two, three or more variables. Linear equations occur with great regularity in applied mathematics.

    a. BDDC
    c. Cubic function
    b. 15 theorem
    d. Linear equation

13.   The _____ is a function in mathematics. The application of this function to a value x is written as exp(x). Equivalently, this can be written in the form e^x, where e is a mathematical constant, the base of the natural logarithm, which equals approximately 2.718281828, and is also known as Euler's number.

    a. ACTRAN
    c. Area hyperbolic functions
    b. Exponential function
    d. Integral part

14.   In mathematics, the simplest case of _____ refers to the study of problems in which one seeks to minimize or maximize a real function by systematically choosing the values of real or integer variables from within an allowed set. This (a scalar real valued objective function) is actually a small subset of this field which comprises a large area of applied mathematics and generalizes to study of means to obtain 'best available' values of some objective function given a defined domain where the elaboration is on the types of functions and the conditions and nature of the objects in the problem domain.

The first _____ technique, which is known as steepest descent, goes back to Gauss.

a. AUSM
b. ALGOR
c. ACTRAN
d. Optimization

15. In geometry, a _____ is a special plane curve generated by the trace of a fixed point on a small circle that rolls within a larger circle. It is comparable to the cycloid but instead of the circle rolling along a line, it rolls within a circle. The red curve is a _____ traced as the smaller black circle rolls around inside the larger blue circle (parameters are R=3.0, r=1.0, and so k=3), giving a deltoid.

If the smaller circle has radius r, and the larger circle has radius R = kr, then the parametric equations for the curve can be given by either:

$$x(\theta) = (R-r)\cos\theta + r\cos\left(\frac{R-r}{r}\theta\right)$$
$$y(\theta) = (R-r)\sin\theta - r\sin\left(\frac{R-r}{r}\theta\right),$$

or:

$$x(\theta) = r(k-1)\cos\theta + r\cos((k-1)\theta)$$
$$y(\theta) = r(k-1)\sin\theta - r\sin((k-1)\theta).$$

If k is an integer, then the curve is closed, and has k cusps (i.e., sharp corners, where the curve is not differentiable.)

a. Kappa curve
b. Closed curve
c. Hypocycloid
d. Bullet-nose curve

16. In mathematics and its applications, _____ refers to finding the linear approximation to a function at a given point. In the study of dynamical systems, _____ is a method for assessing the local stability of an equilibrium point of a system of nonlinear differential equations or discrete dynamical systems. This method is used in fields such as engineering, physics, economics, and ecology.

a. Symmetrically continuous
b. Stationary point
c. Point of inflection
d. Linearization

17. In calculus, an antiderivative, primitive or _____ of a function f is a function F whose derivative is equal to f, i.e., F ' = f. The process of solving for antiderivatives is antidifferentiation (or indefinite integration.) Antiderivatives are related to definite integrals through the fundamental theorem of calculus: the definite integral of a function over an interval is equal to the difference between the values of an antiderivative evaluated at the endpoints of the interval.

a. Integral test for convergence
b. Integration by parts operator
c. Arc length
d. Indefinite integral

18. The _____ of a material is defined as its mass per unit volume. The symbol of _____ is ρ '>rho.)

Mathematically:

$$d = \frac{m}{V}$$

where:

d is the _____,
m is the mass,
V is the volume.

a. BIBO stability
c. 15 theorem

b. BDDC
d. Density

19. _____, linear mass density or linear mass is a measure of mass per unit of length, and it is a characteristic of strings or other one-dimensional objects. The SI unit of _____ is the kilogram per metre (kg/m.) The _____, μ (sometimes denoted by λ), of an object is defined as:

$$\mu = \frac{\partial m}{\partial x}$$

where m is the mass, and x is a coordinate along the (one dimensional) object.

a. Linear density
c. 15 theorem

b. BIBO stability
d. BDDC

20. In physics, and more specifically kinematics, _____ is the change in velocity over time. Because velocity is a vector, it can change in two ways: a change in magnitude and/or a change in direction. In one dimension, _____ is the rate at which something speeds up or slows down.
a. ALGOR
c. AUSM

b. ACTRAN
d. Acceleration

21. In physics, _____ is defined as the rate of change of position. it is vector physical quantity; both speed and direction are required to define it. In the SI (metric) system, it is measured in meters per second: (m/s) or ms^{-1}.
a. Velocity
c. 15 theorem

b. BDDC
d. BIBO stability

22. In mathematics, an _____ is a generalization for the concept of a function in which the dependent variable has not been given 'explicitly' in terms of the independent variable. To give a function f explicitly is to provide a prescription for determining the output value of the function y in terms of the input value x:

y = f(x.)

By contrast, the function is implicit if the value of y is obtained from x by solving an equation of the form:

R(x,y) = 0.

- a. Implicit differentiation
- b. Ordinary differential equation
- c. Automatic differentiation
- d. Implicit Function

23. In the branch of mathematics called multivariable calculus, the _____ is a tool which allows relations to be converted to functions. It does this by representing the relation as the graph of a function. There may not be a single function whose graph is the entire relation, but there may be such a function on a restriction of the domain of the relation.
- a. Inverse function theorem
- b. Isoperimetric inequality
- c. Implicit Function Theorem
- d. Upper convected time derivative

24. In mathematics, a _____ is a constant multiplicative factor of a certain object. For example, in the expression $9x^2$, the _____ of x^2 is 9.

The object can be such things as a variable, a vector, a function, etc.

- a. Leading coefficient
- b. Coefficient
- c. Difference polynomial
- d. Degree of the polynomial

25. The _____ specifies the relationship between the two central operations of calculus, differentiation and integration.

The first part of the theorem, sometimes called the first _____, shows that an indefinite integration can be reversed by a differentiation.

The second part, sometimes called the second _____, allows one to compute the definite integral of a function by using any one of its infinitely many antiderivatives.

- a. Calculus controversy
- b. Minimum
- c. Fundamental Theorem of Calculus
- d. Partial sum

26. Cantor defined two kinds of _____ numbers, the ordinal numbers and the cardinal numbers. Ordinal numbers may be identified with well-ordered sets, or counting carried on to any stopping point, including points after an _____ number have already been counted. Generalizing finite and the ordinary _____ sequences which are maps from the positive integers leads to mappings from ordinal numbers, and transfinite sequences.
- a. ACTRAN
- b. AUSM
- c. Infinite
- d. ALGOR

27. In mathematics, a _____ is an ordered list of objects (or events). Like a set, it contains members (also called elements or terms), and the number of terms (possibly infinite) is called the length of the _____. Unlike a set, order matters, and the exact same elements can appear multiple times at different positions in the _____.

a. BDDC
b. Y-intercept
c. 15 theorem
d. Sequence

28. In calculus, a branch of mathematics, the _____ is a measurement of how a function changes when its input changes. Loosely speaking, a _____ can be thought of as how much a quantity is changing at some given point. For example, the _____ of the position (or distance) of a vehicle with respect to time is the instantaneous velocity (respectively, instantaneous speed) at which the vehicle is traveling.

The process of finding a _____ is called differentiation. The fundamental theorem of calculus states that differentiation is the reverse process to integration.

a. Mountain pass theorem
b. Concave upwards
c. Ramp function
d. Derivative

29. In mathematics, the trigonometric integrals are a family of integrals which involve trigonometric functions. A number of the basic trigonometric integrals are discussed at the list of integrals of trigonometric functions. Plot of Si(x) for 0 ≤ x ≤ 8π.

The different _____ definitions are:

$$\text{Si}(x) = \int_0^x \frac{\sin t}{t} dt$$

$$\text{si}(x) = -\int_x^\infty \frac{\sin t}{t} dt$$

Si(x) is the primitive of sinx / x which is zero for x = 0; si(x) is the primitive of sinx / x which is zero for $x = \infty$.

a. 15 theorem
b. Sine integral
c. Trigonometric integrals
d. Trigonometric

30. In mathematics, a _____ is a basic technique used to simplify problems in which the original variables are replaced with new ones; the new and old variables being related in some specified way. The intent is that the problem expressed in new variables may be simpler, or else equivalent to a better understood problem.

A very simple example of a useful variable change can be seen in the problem of finding the roots of the eighth order polynomial:

$$x^8 + 3x^4 + 2 = 0$$

Eighth order polynomial equations are generally impossible to solve in terms of elementary functions.

a. Cubic function
b. Change of variables
c. BDDC
d. 15 theorem

31. Just as the definite integral of a positive function of one variable represents the area of the region between the graph of the function and the x-axis, the _____ of a positive function of two variables represents the volume of the region between the surface defined by the function (on the three dimensional Cartesian plane where z = f(x,y)) and the plane which contains its domain. (Note that the same volume can be obtained via the triple integral -- the integral of a function in three variables -- of the constant function f(x, y, z) = 1 over the above-mentioned region between the surface and the plane.) If there are more variables, a multiple integral will yield hypervolumes of multi-dimensional functions.

    a. Sum rule in integration   b. Nonelementary integral
    c. Double integral   d. Linearity of integration

32. In calculus, and more generally in mathematical analysis, _____ is a rule that transforms the integral of products of functions into other, hopefully simpler, integrals. The rule arises from the product rule of differentiation.

If u = f(x), v = g(x), and the differentials du = f '(x) dx and dv = g'(x) dx; then in its simplest form the product rule is:

$$\int u\,dv = uv - \int v\,du.$$

Suppose f(x) and g(x) are two continuously differentiable functions.

    a. Integration by parts   b. Integration by parametric derivatives
    c. Arc length   d. Integrand

33. However, in algebra and in particular in algebraic combinatorics, the term '_____' is often used instead to refer to elements of the ring of symmetric functions, where that ring is a specific limit of the rings of symmetric polynomials in n indeterminates, as n goes to infinity. This ring serves as universal structure in which relations between symmetric polynomials can be expressed in a way independent of the number n of indeterminates (but its elements are neither polynomials nor functions.) Among other things, this ring plays an important role in the representation theory of the symmetric groups.

    a. Leading coefficient   b. Symmetric function
    c. Binomial type   d. Difference polynomial

34. _____ generally conveys two primary meanings. The first is an imprecise sense of harmonious or aesthetically-pleasing proportionality and balance; such that it reflects beauty or perfection. The second meaning is a precise and well-defined concept of balance or 'patterned self-similarity' that can be demonstrated or proved according to the rules of a formal system: by geometry, through physics or otherwise.

    a. BDDC   b. Symmetry
    c. 15 theorem   d. BIBO stability

35. Call S_N the _____ to N of the sequence $\{a_n\}$, or _____ of the series. A series is the sequence of partial sums, $\{S_N\}$.

When talking about series, one can refer either to the sequence $\{S_N\}$ of the partial sums, or to the sum of the series,

$$\sum_{n=0}^{\infty} a_n$$

i.e., the limit of the sequence of partial sums - it is clear which one is meant from context.

a. Minimum
b. Partial sum
c. Root test
d. Periodic function

36. In mathematics, _____ refers to the rewriting of an expression into a simpler form. For example, the process of rewriting a fraction into one with the smallest whole-number denominator possible (while keeping the numerator an integer) is called 'reducing a fraction'. Rewriting a radical (or 'root') expression with the smallest possible whole number under the radical symbol is called 'reducing a radical'.

a. 15 theorem
b. BDDC
c. BIBO stability
d. Reduction

37. Trigonometry is a branch of mathematics that deals with triangles, particularly those plane triangles in which one angle has 90 degrees (right triangles.) Trigonometry deals with relationships between the sides and the angles of triangles and with the _____ functions, which describe those relationships.

Trigonometry has applications in both pure mathematics and in applied mathematics, where it is essential in many branches of science and technology.

a. 15 theorem
b. Trigonometric functions
c. Trigonometric integrals
d. Trigonometric

38. In mathematics, the _____ are functions of an angle. They are important in the study of triangles and modeling periodic phenomena, among many other applications. _____ are commonly defined as ratios of two sides of a right triangle containing the angle, and can equivalently be defined as the lengths of various line segments from a unit circle.

a. Trigonometric integrals
b. Trigonometric
c. 15 theorem
d. Trigonometric functions

39. In mathematics, the _____ are a family of integrals which involve trigonometric functions. A number of the basic _____ are discussed at the list of integrals of trigonometric functions.

The different sine integral definitions are:

$$\text{Si}(x) = \int_0^x \frac{\sin t}{t}\, dt$$

$$\text{si}(x) = -\int_x^\infty \frac{\sin t}{t}\, dt$$

Si(x) is the primitive of sinx / x which is zero for x = 0; si(x) is the primitive of sinx / x which is zero for $x = \infty$.

a. 15 theorem
b. Trigonometric
c. Trigonometric functions
d. Trigonometric integrals

40. In mathematics, _____ is the substitution of trigonometric functions for other expressions. One may use the trigonometric identities to simplify certain integrals containing radical expressions:

- If the integrand contains

$$\sqrt{a^2 - x^2},$$

let

$$x = a \sin \theta$$

and use the identity

$1 - \sin^2\theta = \cos^2\theta.$

- If the integrand contains

$$\sqrt{a^2 + x^2}$$

let $x = a \tan \theta$
and use the identity

$$1 + \tan^2 \theta = \sec^2 \theta.$$

- If the integrand contains

$$\sqrt{x^2 - a^2}$$

let

$$x = a\sec\theta$$

and use the identity

$$\sec^2\theta - 1 = \tan^2\theta.$$

In the integral

$$\int \frac{dx}{\sqrt{a^2 - x^2}}$$

we may use

$$x = a\sin(\theta), \; dx = a\cos(\theta)\,d\theta$$
$$\theta = \arcsin\left(\frac{x}{a}\right)$$

so that the integral becomes

$$\int \frac{dx}{\sqrt{a^2 - x^2}} = \int \frac{a\cos(\theta)\,d\theta}{\sqrt{a^2 - a^2\sin^2(\theta)}} = \int \frac{a\cos(\theta)\,d\theta}{\sqrt{a^2(1 - \sin^2(\theta))}}$$
$$= \int \frac{a\cos(\theta)\,d\theta}{\sqrt{a^2\cos^2(\theta)}} = \int d\theta = \theta + C = \arcsin\left(\frac{x}{a}\right) + C$$

Note that the above step requires that a > 0 and cos(θ) > 0; we can choose the a to be the positive square root of a^2; and we impose the restriction on θ to be −π/2 < θ < π/2 by using the arcsin function.

For a definite integral, one must figure out how the bounds of integration change. For example, as x goes from 0 to a/2, then sin (θ) goes from 0 to 1/2, so θ goes from 0 to π/6.

a. Signed measure
c. Trigonometric substitution
b. Surface of revolution
d. Linearity of integration

41. In integral calculus we would want to write a fractional algebraic expression as the sum of its _____ in order to take the integral of each simple fraction separately. Once the original denominator, D_0, has been factored we set up a fraction for each factor in the denominator. We may use a subscripted D to represent the denominator of the respective _____ which are the factors in D_0.

a. Hurwitz quaternion order
c. Completing the square
b. Partial fractions
d. Multinomial theorem

42. In economics, the _____ functional form of production functions is widely used to represent the relationship of an output to inputs. It was proposed by Knut Wicksell (1851-1926), and tested against statistical evidence by Charles Cobb and Paul Douglas in 1900-1928.

For production, the function is

$$Y = AL^{\alpha}K^{\beta},$$

where:

- Y = total production (the monetary value of all goods produced in a year)
- L = labor input
- K = capital input
- A = total factor productivity
- α and β are the output elasticities of labor and capital, respectively. These values are constants determined by available technology.

Output elasticity measures the responsiveness of output to a change in levels of either labor or capital used in production, ceteris paribus. For example if α = 0.15, a 1% increase in labor would lead to approximately a 0.15% increase in output.

a. BIBO stability
b. BDDC
c. 15 theorem
d. Cobb-Douglas

43. In mathematics, an _____ is a function built from a finite number of exponentials, logarithms, constants, one variable, and nth roots through composition and combinations using the four elementary operations (+ - × ÷.) The trigonometric functions and their inverses are assumed to be included in the elementary functions by using complex variables and the relations between the trigonometric functions and the exponential and logarithm functions.

Elementary functions are considered a subset of special functions.

a. AUSM
b. ALGOR
c. ACTRAN
d. Elementary function

44. In mathematics and physics, the _____ or Laplacian, denoted by Δ or ∇^2 and named after Pierre-Simon de Laplace, is a differential operator, specifically an important case of an elliptic operator, with many applications. In physics, it is used in modeling of wave propagation, heat flow and forming the Helmholtz equation. It is central in electrostatics and fluid mechanics, anchoring in Laplace's equation and Poisson's equation.

a. Laplace operator
b. Vector Laplacian
c. Partial derivative
d. Differentiation operator

45. In statistics, _____ is a form of regression analysis in which the relationship between one or more independent variables and another variable, called dependent variable, is modeled by a least squares function, called _____ equation. This function is a linear combination of one or more model parameters, called regression coefficients. A _____ equation with one independent variable represents a straight line.

Chapter 5. Integrals

a. Linear regression
b. Poisson distribution
c. Standard deviation
d. Normal distribution

46. In numerical analysis, _____ constitutes a broad family of algorithms for calculating the numerical value of a definite integral, and by extension, the term is also sometimes used to describe the numerical solution of differential equations The term numerical quadrature is more or less a synonym for _____, especially as applied to one-dimensional integrals.

a. Multigrid method
b. Galerkin methods
c. Meshfree methods
d. Numerical integration

47. In mathematics, the _____ is a way to approximately calculate the definite integral

$$\int_a^b f(x)\,dx.$$

The _____ works by approximating the region under the graph of the function f by a trapezoid and calculating its area. It follows that

$$\int_a^b f(x)\,dx \approx (b-a)\frac{f(a)+f(b)}{2}.$$

To calculate this integral more accurately, one first splits the interval of integration [a,b] into n smaller subintervals, and then applies the _____ on each of them. One obtains the composite _____:

$$\int_a^b f(x)\,dx \approx \frac{b-a}{n}\left[\frac{f(a)+f(b)}{2} + \sum_{k=1}^{n-1} f\left(a + k\frac{b-a}{n}\right)\right].$$

This can alternatively be written as:

$$\int_a^b f(x)\,dx \approx \frac{b-a}{2n}\left(f(x_0) + 2f(x_1) + 2f(x_2) + \cdots + 2f(x_{n-1}) + f(x_n)\right)$$

where

$$x_k = a + k\frac{b-a}{n}, \text{ for } k = 0, 1, \ldots, n$$

(one can also use a non-uniform grid.)

a. BDDC
b. 15 theorem
c. Trapezoidal Rule
d. BIBO stability

48. In mathematics, an _____ is an infinite series of the form

Chapter 5. Integrals

$$\sum_{n=0}^{\infty} (-1)^n a_n,$$

with $a_n \geq 0$ (or $a_n \leq 0$) for all n. A finite sum of this kind is an alternating sum. An _____ converges if the terms a_n converge to 0 monotonically.

- a. Uniform convergence
- b. Infinite series
- c. Extreme value
- d. Alternating series

49. The _____ is a doubly ruled surface shaped like a saddle. In a suitable coordinate system, it can be represented by the equation

$$z = \frac{x^2}{a^2} - \frac{y^2}{b^2}.$$

This is a _____ that opens up along the x-axis and down along the y-axis.

Paraboloid of revolution

With a = b an elliptic paraboloid is a paraboloid of revolution: a surface obtained by revolving a parabola around its axis.

- a. PDE surfaces
- b. Parametric surface
- c. Hyperbolic paraboloid
- d. Prolate

50. In calculus, an _____ is the limit of a definite integral as an endpoint of the interval of integration approaches either a specified real number or ∞ or −∞ or, in some cases, as both endpoints approach limits.

Specifically, an _____ is a limit of the form

$$\lim_{b \to \infty} \int_a^b f(x)\,dx, \qquad \lim_{a \to -\infty} \int_a^b f(x)\,dx,$$

or of the form

$$\lim_{c \to b^-} \int_a^c f(x)\,dx, \qquad \lim_{c \to a^+} \int_c^b f(x)\,dx,$$

in which one takes a limit in one or the other (or sometimes both) endpoints . Improper integrals may also occur at an interior point of the domain of integration, or at multiple such points.

a. AUSM
b. ALGOR
c. ACTRAN
d. Improper integral

51. In mathematics, a _____ is a quadric surface of special kind. There are two kinds of paraboloids: elliptic and hyperbolic. The elliptic _____ is shaped like an oval cup and can have a maximum or minimum point.
   a. Normal line
   b. Parametric surface
   c. Normal vector
   d. Paraboloid

52. In vector calculus, the _____ is an operator that measures the magnitude of a vector field's source or sink at a given point; the _____ of a vector field is a (signed) scalar. For example, consider air as it is heated or cooled. The relevant vector field for this example is the velocity of the moving air at a point.
   a. Divergence Theorem
   b. Triple product
   c. Gradient theorem
   d. Divergence

53. A _____ is a model used within physics to explain how gravity exists in the universe. In its original concept, gravity was a force between point masses. Following Newton, Laplace attempted to model gravity as some kind of radiation field or fluid, and since the 19th century explanations for gravity have usually been sought in terms of a field model, rather than a point attraction.
   a. Gravitational field
   b. BIBO stability
   c. 15 theorem
   d. BDDC

54. In mathematics, a _____ is an approximation of a general function using a linear function (more precisely, an affine function.)

Given a differentiable function f of one real variable, Taylor's theorem for n=1 states that

$$f(x) = f(a) + f\,'(a)(x-a) + R_2$$

where R_2 is the remainder term. The _____ is obtained by dropping the remainder:

$$f(x) \approx f(a) + f\,'(a)(x-a)$$

which is true for x close to a.

   a. Smooth function
   b. Differentiation of trigonometric functions
   c. Linearity of differentiation
   d. Linear approximation

55. In probability theory and statistics, the _____ (or expectation value or mean and for continuous random variables with a density function it is the probability density -weighted integral of the possible values.

The term '_____' can be misleading.

   a. AUSM
   b. Expected value
   c. ACTRAN
   d. ALGOR

Chapter 6. Applications of Integration

1. A _____ is the portion of a solid--normally a cone or pyramid--which lies between two parallel planes cutting the solid. The term is commonly used in computer graphics to describe the 3d area which is visible on the screen (which is formed by a clipped pyramid.)

Each plane section is a base of the _____.

   a. Frustum
   b. BDDC
   c. BIBO stability
   d. 15 theorem

2. In mathematics, a (topological) _____ is defined as follows: let I be an interval of real numbers (i.e. a non-empty connected subset of $\mathbb{R}$); then a _____ γ is a continuous mapping $\gamma : I \to X$, where X is a topological space. The _____ γ is said to be simple if it is injective, i.e. if for all x, y in I, we have $\gamma(x) = \gamma(y) \implies x = y$. If I is a closed bounded interval $[a, b]$, we also allow the possibility $\gamma(a) = \gamma(b)$ (this convention makes it possible to talk about closed simple _____.)

   a. Curve
   b. Prolate cycloid
   c. Tractrix
   d. Closed curve

3. In mathematics, _____ are a method of defining a curve. A simple kinematical example is when one uses a time parameter to determine the position, velocity, and other information about a body in motion.

Abstractly, a relation is given in the form of an equation, and it is shown also to be the image of functions from items such as R^n.

   a. Laplace operator
   b. Differential operator
   c. Parametric equations
   d. Multivariable calculus

4. In mathematics, the hyperbolic functions are analogs of the ordinary trigonometric functions. The basic hyperbolic functions are the hyperbolic sine 'sinh', and the _____ 'cosh', from which are derived the hyperbolic tangent 'tanh', etc., in analogy to the derived trigonometric functions. The inverse hyperbolic functions are the area hyperbolic sine 'arsinh' (also called 'asinh', or sometimes by the misnomer of 'arcsinh') and so on.

   a. Heaviside step function
   b. Hyperbolic cosine
   c. Signum function
   d. Multiplicative inverse

5. In common usage, a cylinder is taken to mean a finite section of a right _____ with its ends closed to form two circular surfaces, as in the figure (right.) If the cylinder has a radius r and length (height) h, then its volume is given by

$$V = \pi r^2 h$$

and its surface area is:

- the area of the top (πr^2) +
- the area of the bottom (πr^2) +
- the area of the side $(2\pi r h)$.

Therefore without the top or bottom (lateral area), the surface area is

$$A = 2\pi r h.$$

With the top and bottom, the surface area is

$$A = 2\pi r^2 + 2\pi r h = 2\pi r(r + h).$$

For a given volume, the cylinder with the smallest surface area has h = 2r. For a given surface area, the cylinder with the largest volume has h = 2r, i.e. the cylinder fits in a cube (height = diameter.)

Cylindric sections are the intersections of cylinders with planes.

a. 15 theorem
b. BDDC
c. Cylinder
d. Circular cylinder

6. A _____ is one of the most curvilinear basic geometric shapes:It has two faces, zero vertices, and zero edges. The surface formed by the points at a fixed distance from a given straight line, the axis of the _____. The solid enclosed by this surface and by two planes perpendicular to the axis is also called a _____.

a. 15 theorem
b. Right circular cylinder
c. Cylinder
d. BDDC

7. In common usage, a cylinder is taken to mean a finite section of a _____ with its ends closed to form two circular surfaces, as in the figure (right.) If the cylinder has a radius r and length (height) h, then its volume is given by

$$V = \pi r^2 h$$

and its surface area is:

- the area of the top (πr^2) +
- the area of the bottom (πr^2) +
- the area of the side $(2\pi r h)$.

Therefore without the top or bottom (lateral area), the surface area is

$$A = 2\pi r h.$$

With the top and bottom, the surface area is

$$A = 2\pi r^2 + 2\pi r h = 2\pi r(r + h).$$

For a given volume, the cylinder with the smallest surface area has h = 2r. For a given surface area, the cylinder with the largest volume has h = 2r, i.e. the cylinder fits in a cube (height = diameter.)

Cylindric sections are the intersections of cylinders with planes.

- a. Right circular cylinder
- b. Cylinder
- c. 15 theorem
- d. BDDC

8. In mathematics, engineering, and manufacturing, a _____ is a solid figure obtained by rotating a plane curve around some straight line (the axis) that lies on the same plane.

Assuming that the curve does not cross the axis, the solid's volume is equal to the length of the circle described by the figure's centroid, times the figure's area (Pappus's second centroid Theorem.)

Rotating a curve

A representative disk is a three-dimensional volume element of a _____.

- a. Riemann sum
- b. Risch algorithm
- c. Sum rule in integration
- d. Solid of revolution

9. In geometry, a _____ is a three-dimensional figure formed by six parallelograms. It is to a parallelogram as a cube is to a square: Euclidean geometry supports all four notions but affine geometry admits only parallelograms and parallelepipeds. Three equivalent definitions of _____ are

- a polyhedron with six faces (hexahedron), each of which is a parallelogram,
- a hexahedron with three pairs of parallel faces, and
- a prism of which the base is a parallelogram.

The cuboid (six rectangular faces), cube (six square faces), and the rhombohedron (six rhombus faces) are all specific cases of _____.

Parallelepipeds are a subclass of the prismatoids.

a. BDDC
b. BIBO stability
c. Parallelepiped
d. 15 theorem

10. _____ is a means of calculating the volume of a solid of revolution, when integrating along the axis of revolution. This method models the generated 3 dimensional shape as a 'stack' of an infinite number of disks of infinitesimal thickness. It is possible to use 'washers' instead of 'disks' (the washer method) to obtain 'hollow' solids of revolutions, and uses the same principles that underlie _____.

a. Multiple integral
b. Shell integration
c. Surface of revolution
d. Disk integration

11. In geometry, a _____ (pl. tori) is a surface of revolution generated by revolving a circle in three dimensional space about an axis coplanar with the circle, which does not touch the circle. Examples of tori include the surfaces of doughnuts and inner tubes.

a. Prolate
b. PDE surfaces
c. Normal vector
d. Torus

12. For some curves there is a smallest number L that is an upper bound on the length of any polygonal approximation. If such a number exists, then the curve is said to be rectifiable and the curve is defined to have _____ L.

Let C be a curve in Euclidean (or, generally, a metric) space $X = R^n$, so C is the image of a continuous function $f : [a, b] \to X$ of the interval [a, b] into X.

a. Arc length
b. Integration by parametric derivatives
c. Integrand
d. Order of integration

13. A _____ is a type of manifold that is locally similar enough to Euclidean space to allow one to do calculus Any manifold can be described by a collection of charts, also known as an atlas.

a. Minimal surface
b. Tortuosity
c. Lie derivative
d. Differentiable manifold

14. In probability theory and statistics, the _____ (or expectation value or mean and for continuous random variables with a density function it is the probability density -weighted integral of the possible values.

The term '_____' can be misleading.

a. ALGOR
b. ACTRAN
c. AUSM
d. Expected value

15. In calculus, the _____ states, roughly, that given a section of a smooth curve, there is at least one point on that section at which the derivative (slope) of the curve is equal (parallel) to the 'average' derivative of the section. It is used to prove theorems that make global conclusions about a function on an interval starting from local hypotheses about derivatives at points of the interval.

This theorem can be understood concretely by applying it to motion: If a car travels one hundred miles in one hour, so its average speed during that time was 100 miles per hour.

a. Fresnel integrals
b. First derivative test
c. Mean Value Theorem
d. Leibniz differential

16. Integration is an important concept in mathematics, specifically in the field of calculus and, more broadly, mathematical analysis. Given a function f of a real variable x and an interval [a, b] of the real line, the _____

$$\int_a^b f(x)\, dx,$$

is defined informally to be the net signed area of the region in the xy-plane bounded by the graph of f, the x-axis, and the vertical lines x = a and x = b.

The term '_____' may also refer to the notion of antiderivative, a function F whose derivative is the given function f.

a. Indefinite integral
b. Integrand
c. Integral test for convergence
d. Integral

17. The _____ is the derived unit of energy in the International System of Units. It is defined as:

$$1\,\mathrm{J} = 1\,\mathrm{kg} \cdot \mathrm{m}^2 \cdot \mathrm{s}^{-2}$$

One _____ is the amount of energy required to perform the following physical actions:

- The work done by a force of one newton travelling through a distance of one metre;
- The work required to move an electric charge of one coulomb through an electrical potential difference of one volt; or one coulomb volt, with the symbol C·V;
- The work done to produce the power of one watt continuously for one second; or one watt second (compare kilowatt hour), with the symbol W·s. Thus a kilowatt hour is 3,600,000 joules or 3.6 megajoules;

1 _____ is equal to:

- 1×10^7 ergs (exactly)
- 1.6022×10^{19} eV (electronvolts)
- 0.2390 cal (gram calories or small calories)
- 2.3901×10^{-4} kcal (kilocalories, kilogram calories, large calories or food calories)
- 9.4782×10^{-4} BTU (British thermal unit)
- 0.7376 ftÂ·lbf (foot-pound force)
- 23.7 ftÂ·pdl (foot-poundals)
- 2.7778×10^{-7} kilowatt-hour
- 2.7778×10^{-4} watt-hour
- 9.8692×10^{-3} litre-atmosphere
- 1×10^{-44} Foe (exactly)

Units defined in terms of the _____ include:

- 1 thermochemical calorie = 4.184 J
- 1 International Table calorie = 4.1868 J
- 1 watt hour = 3600 J
- 1 kilowatt hour = 3.6×10^6 J (or 3.6 MJ)
- 1 ton TNT exploding = 4.184 GJ

Useful to remember:

- 1 _____ = 1 newton × 1 meter = 1 watt × 1 second

One _____ in everyday life is approximately:

- the energy required to lift a small apple one metre straight up.
- the energy released when that same apple falls one meter to the ground.
- the energy released as heat by a quiet person, every hundredth of a second.
- the energy required to heat one gram of dry, cool air by 1 degree Celsius.
- one hundredth of the energy a person can receive by drinking a drop of beer.
- the kinetic energy of an adult human moving a distance of about a handspan every second.

- Conversion of units
- Orders of magnitude (energy)
- Fluence

a. 15 theorem
b. BDDC
c. BIBO stability
d. Joule

18. In physics, and more specifically kinematics, _____ is the change in velocity over time. Because velocity is a vector, it can change in two ways: a change in magnitude and/or a change in direction. In one dimension, _____ is the rate at which something speeds up or slows down.

a. ALGOR
b. AUSM
c. ACTRAN
d. Acceleration

19. The most commonly encountered form of Hooke's law is probably the spring equation, which relates the force exerted by a spring to the distance it is stretched by a _____, k, measured in force per length.

$$F = -kx$$

The negative sign indicates that the force exerted by the spring is in direct opposition to the direction of displacement. It is called a 'restoring force', as it tends to restore the system to equilibrium.

a. 15 theorem
b. Spring constant
c. Navier-Stokes equations
d. Polar moment of inertia

20. The _____ of a material is defined as its mass per unit volume. The symbol of _____ is ρ '>rho.)

Mathematically:

$$d = \frac{m}{V}$$

where:

d is the _____,
m is the mass,
V is the volume.

a. 15 theorem
b. BIBO stability
c. BDDC
d. Density

21. The concept of _____ in mathematics evolved from the concept of _____ in physics. The nth _____ of a real-valued function f(x) of a real variable about a value c is

$$\mu'_n = \int_{-\infty}^{\infty} (x-c)^n f(x)\,dx.$$

It is possible to define moments for random variables in a more general fashion than moments for real values. See Moments in metric spaces.

Chapter 6. Applications of Integration

a. Linear regression
c. Standard deviation
b. Moment
d. Poisson distribution

22. _____ generally conveys two primary meanings. The first is an imprecise sense of harmonious or aesthetically-pleasing proportionality and balance; such that it reflects beauty or perfection. The second meaning is a precise and well-defined concept of balance or 'patterned self-similarity' that can be demonstrated or proved according to the rules of a formal system: by geometry, through physics or otherwise.

a. 15 theorem
c. Symmetry
b. BIBO stability
d. BDDC

23. The mechanisms of _____; a point mass m_1 attracts another point mass m_2 by a force F_2 which is proportional to the product of the two masses and inversely proportional to the square of the distance (r) between them. Regardless of masses or distance, the magnitudes of $|F_1|$ and $|F_2|$ will always be equal. G is the gravitational constant.

_____ is an empirical physical law describing the gravitational attraction between bodies with mass.

a. BDDC
c. BIBO stability
b. 15 theorem
d. Newton's law of universal gravitation

24. In the various subfields of physics, there exist two common usages of the term _____, both with rigorous mathematical frameworks.

- In the study of transport phenomena (heat transfer, mass transfer and fluid dynamics), _____ is defined as the amount that flows through a unit area per unit time. _____ in this definition is a vector.
- In the field of electromagnetism and mathematics, _____ is usually the integral of a vector quantity over a finite surface. The result of this integration is a scalar quantity. The magnetic _____ is thus the integral of the magnetic vector field B over a surface, and the electric _____ is defined similarly. Using this definition, the _____ of the Poynting vector over a specified surface is the rate at which electromagnetic energy flows through that surface. Confusingly, the Poynting vector is sometimes called the power _____, which is an example of the first usage of _____, above. It has units of watts per square metre (WÂ·m^{-2})

One could argue, based on the work of James Clerk Maxwell, that the transport definition precedes the more recent way the term is used in electromagnetism. The specific quote from Maxwell is 'In the case of fluxes, we have to take the integral, over a surface, of the _____ through every element of the surface. The result of this operation is called the surface integral of the _____.

a. BDDC
c. 15 theorem
b. BIBO stability
d. Flux

25. In probability theory, a probability distribution is called continuous if its cumulative distribution function is continuous. This is equivalent to saying that for random variables X with the distribution in question, Pr[X = a] = 0 for all real numbers a, i.e.: the probability that X attains the value a is zero, for any number a. If the distribution of X is continuous then X is called a _____.

a. Linear regression
c. Standard deviation
b. Continuous random variable
d. Moment

26. In mathematics, a _____ (pdf) is a function that represents a probability distribution in terms of integrals.

Formally, a probability distribution has density f, if f is a non-negative Lebesgue-integrable function $\mathbb{R} \to \mathbb{R}$ such that the probability of the interval [a, b] is given by

$$\int_a^b f(x)\,dx$$

for any two numbers a and b. This implies that the total integral of f must be 1.

a. BIBO stability
b. BDDC
c. Probability density function
d. 15 theorem

27. The _____ is an important family of continuous probability distributions, applicable in many fields. Each member of the family may be defined by two parameters, location and scale: the mean and variance respectively. The standard _____ is the _____ with a mean of zero and a variance of one.

a. Normal distribution
b. Linear regression
c. Continuous random variable
d. Poisson distribution

28. In statistics, _____ is a simple measure of the variability or dispersion of a data set. A low _____ indicates that all of the data points are very close to the same value (the mean), while high _____ indicates that the data is 'spread out' over a large range of values.

For example, the average height for adult men in the United States is about 70 inches, with a _____ of around 3 inches.

a. Poisson distribution
b. Moment
c. Normal distribution
d. Standard deviation

Chapter 7. Differential Equations

1. In infinitesimal calculus, a _____ is traditionally an infinitesimally small change in a variable. For example, if x is a variable, then a change in the value of x is often denoted Δx (or δx when this change is considered to be small.) The _____ dx represents such a change, but is infinitely small.

   a. Differential
   b. Related rates
   c. Dirichlet integral
   d. Continuous function

2. A _____ is a mathematical equation for an unknown function of one or several variables that relates the values of the function itself and of its derivatives of various orders. they play a prominent role in engineering, physics, economics and other disciplines.

   A simplified real world example of a _____ is modeling the acceleration of a ball falling through the air (considering only gravity and air resistance.)

   a. Structural stability
   b. Petrovsky lacuna
   c. Differential equation
   d. Lax pair

3. A _____ or Gompertz function, named after Benjamin Gompertz, is a sigmoid function. It is a type of mathematical model for a time series, where growth is slowest at the start and end of a time period. Graphs of Gompertz curves, showing the effect of varying one of a,b,c while keeping the others constant.

$$y(t) = ae^{be^{ct}}$$

where

- a is the upper asymptote
- c is the growth rate
- b, c are negative numbers
- e is Euler's Number (e = 2.71828...)

The function curve can be derived from Gompertz's law, which states the rate of mortality (decay) falls exponentially with current size. Mathematically

$$k^r \propto \frac{1}{y(t)}$$

where

- $r = \frac{y'(t)}{y(t)}$ is the rate of growth.
- k is an arbitrary constant.

Chapter 7. Differential Equations

Examples of uses for Gompertz curves include:

- Mobile phone uptake, where costs were initially high (so uptake was slow), followed by a period of rapid growth, followed by a slowing of uptake as saturation was reached.
- Population in a confined space, as birth rates first increase and then slow as resource limits are reached.
- Modeling of growth of tumors

In the sixties A.K. Laird for the first time successfully used the _____ to fit data of growth of tumors. In fact, tumors are cellular populations growing in a confined space where the availability of nutrients is limited.

a. Duffing equation
b. Spheroidal wave functions
c. Neumann-Dirichlet method
d. Gompertz curve

4. In mathematics, engineering, and manufacturing, a _____ is a solid figure obtained by rotating a plane curve around some straight line (the axis) that lies on the same plane.

Assuming that the curve does not cross the axis, the solid's volume is equal to the length of the circle described by the figure's centroid, times the figure's area (Pappus's second centroid Theorem.)

Rotating a curve

A representative disk is a three-dimensional volume element of a _____.

a. Sum rule in integration
b. Riemann sum
c. Risch algorithm
d. Solid of revolution

5. The most commonly encountered form of Hooke's law is probably the spring equation, which relates the force exerted by a spring to the distance it is stretched by a _____, k, measured in force per length.

$$F = -kx$$

The negative sign indicates that the force exerted by the spring is in direct opposition to the direction of displacement. It is called a 'restoring force', as it tends to restore the system to equilibrium.

a. Spring constant
b. Polar moment of inertia
c. 15 theorem
d. Navier-Stokes equations

6. In mathematics, in the field of differential equations, an initial value problem is an ordinary differential equation together with specified value, called the _____, of the unknown function at a given point in the domain of the solution. In physics or other sciences, modeling a system frequently amounts to solving an initial value problem; in this context, the differential equation is an evolution equation specifying how, given initial conditions, the system will evolve with time.

An initial value problem is a differential equation

$$y'(t) = f(t, y(t)) \quad \text{with} \quad f : \mathbb{R} \times \mathbb{R} \to \mathbb{R}$$

together with a point in the domain of f

$$(t_0, y_0) \in \mathbb{R} \times \mathbb{R},$$

called the _____.

   a. Initial condition   b. ACTRAN
   c. AUSM   d. ALGOR

7. In mathematics, in the field of differential equations, an _____ is an ordinary differential equation together with specified value, called the initial condition, of the unknown function at a given point in the domain of the solution. In physics or other sciences, modeling a system frequently amounts to solving an _____; in this context, the differential equation is an evolution equation specifying how, given initial conditions, the system will evolve with time.

An _____ is a differential equation

$$y'(t) = f(t, y(t)) \quad \text{with} \quad f : \mathbb{R} \times \mathbb{R} \to \mathbb{R}$$

together with a point in the domain of f

$$(t_0, y_0) \in \mathbb{R} \times \mathbb{R},$$

called the initial condition.

   a. ACTRAN   b. ALGOR
   c. AUSM   d. Initial value problem

8. In geometry, an _____ is a plane curve produced by tracing the path of a chosen point of a circle -- called epicycle -- which rolls without slipping around a fixed circle. It is a particular kind of roulette.

If the smaller circle has radius r, and the larger circle has radius R = kr, then the parametric equations for the curve can be given by either:

$$x(\theta) = (R + r) \cos \theta - r \cos \left(\frac{R + r}{r} \theta \right)$$
$$y(\theta) = (R + r) \sin \theta - r \sin \left(\frac{R + r}{r} \theta \right),$$

or:

$$x(\theta) = r(k+1)\cos\theta - r\cos((k+1)\theta)$$
$$y(\theta) = r(k+1)\sin\theta - r\sin((k+1)\theta).$$

If k is an integer, then the curve is closed, and has k cusps (i.e., sharp corners, where the curve is not differentiable.)

a. Asymptotic curve
b. ACTRAN
c. ALGOR
d. Epicycloid

9. In mathematics, a _____ to an ordinary or partial differential equation is a function for which the derivatives appearing in the equation may not all exist but which is nonetheless deemed to satisfy the equation in some precisely defined sense. There are many different definitions of _____, appropriate for different classes of equations. One of the most important is based on the notion of distributions.

a. Singular perturbation
b. Nahm equations
c. Riemann-Hilbert correspondence
d. Weak solution

10. In geometry, a _____ is a special plane curve generated by the trace of a fixed point on a small circle that rolls within a larger circle. It is comparable to the cycloid but instead of the circle rolling along a line, it rolls within a circle. The red curve is a _____ traced as the smaller black circle rolls around inside the larger blue circle (parameters are R=3.0, r=1.0, and so k=3), giving a deltoid.

If the smaller circle has radius r, and the larger circle has radius R = kr, then the parametric equations for the curve can be given by either:

$$x(\theta) = (R-r)\cos\theta + r\cos\left(\frac{R-r}{r}\theta\right)$$
$$y(\theta) = (R-r)\sin\theta - r\sin\left(\frac{R-r}{r}\theta\right),$$

or:

$$x(\theta) = r(k-1)\cos\theta + r\cos((k-1)\theta)$$
$$y(\theta) = r(k-1)\sin\theta - r\sin((k-1)\theta).$$

If k is an integer, then the curve is closed, and has k cusps (i.e., sharp corners, where the curve is not differentiable.)

a. Hypocycloid
b. Kappa curve
c. Closed curve
d. Bullet-nose curve

11. In mathematics, a _____ (or direction field) is a graphical representation of the solutions of a first-order differential equation. It is achieved without solving the differential equation analytically, and thence it is useful. The representation may be used to qualitatively visualise solutions, or to numerically approximate them.

   a. The Method of Mechanical Theorems
   b. Standard part function
   c. Fresnel integrals
   d. Slope field

12. In mathematics, a (topological) _____ is defined as follows: let I be an interval of real numbers (i.e. a non-empty connected subset of $\mathbb{R}$); then a _____ γ is a continuous mapping $\gamma : I \to X$, where X is a topological space. The _____ γ is said to be simple if it is injective, i.e. if for all x, y in I, we have $\gamma(x) = \gamma(y) \implies x = y$. If I is a closed bounded interval $[a, b]$, we also allow the possibility $\gamma(a) = \gamma(b)$ (this convention makes it possible to talk about closed simple _____.)

   a. Tractrix
   b. Closed curve
   c. Prolate cycloid
   d. Curve

13. In mathematics, an autonomous system or _____ is a system of ordinary differential equations which does not depend on the independent variable.

Many laws in physics, where the independent variable is usually assumed to be time, are expressed as autonomous systems because it is assumed the laws of nature which hold now are identical to those for any point in the past or future.

Autonomous systems are closely related to dynamical systems.

   a. Algebraic differential equation
   b. Annihilator method
   c. Integro-differential equation
   d. Autonomous Differential equation

14. In mathematics, a _____ differential equation may refer to one of two related things, both of which are differential equations that can be attacked by a method of separation of variables.

- For ordinary differential equations, it describes a class of equations that can be separated into a pair of integrals. See: Examples of differential equations

- For partial differential equations, it describes a class of equations that can be broken down into differential equations in fewer independent variables. See _____ partial differential equation.

   a. Conserved quantity
   b. Lax pair
   c. Separable
   d. Weak solution

15. In mathematics, two vectors are _____ if they are perpendicular, i.e., they form a right angle. For example, a subway and the street above, although they do not physically intersect, are _____ if they cross at a right angle.

   a. ALGOR
   b. Orthogonal
   c. ACTRAN
   d. AUSM

Chapter 7. Differential Equations

16. In mathematics, _____ are a family of curves in the plane that intersect a given family of curves at right angles. The problem is classical, but is now understood by means of complex analysis; see for example harmonic conjugate.

For a family of level curves described by g(x,y) = C, where C is a constant, the _____ may be found as the level curves of a new function f(x,y) by solving the partial differential equation

$$\nabla f \cdot \nabla g = 0$$

for f(x,y).

- a. Orthogonal trajectories
- b. AUSM
- c. ACTRAN
- d. ALGOR

17. A _____ is the path a moving object follows through space. The object might be a projectile or a satellite, for example. It thus includes the meaning of orbit - the path of a planet, an asteroid or a comet as it travels around a central mass.
- a. Trajectory
- b. 15 theorem
- c. BIBO stability
- d. BDDC

18. In physics, _____ is defined as the rate of change of position. it is vector physical quantity; both speed and direction are required to define it. In the SI (metric) system, it is measured in meters per second: (m/s) or ms^{-1}.
- a. BDDC
- b. 15 theorem
- c. BIBO stability
- d. Velocity

19. A quantity is said to be subject to _____ if it decreases at a rate proportional to its value. Symbolically, this can be expressed as the following differential equation, where N is the quantity and λ is a positive number called the decay constant.

$$\frac{dN}{dt} = -\lambda N.$$

The solution to this equation is:

$$N(t) = N_0 e^{-\lambda t}.$$

Here N(t) is the quantity at time t, and N_0 = N(0) is the initial quantity, i.e. the quantity at time t = 0.

- a. ALGOR
- b. ACTRAN
- c. Exponential sum
- d. Exponential decay

20. _____ (including exponential decay) occurs when the growth rate of a mathematical function is proportional to the function's current value. In the case of a discrete domain of definition with equal intervals it is also called geometric growth or geometric decay (the function values form a geometric progression.)

_____ is said to follow an exponential law; the simple-_____ model is known as the Malthusian growth model.

a. Inseparable differential equation
b. Exponential growth
c. Oscillating
d. Isomonodromic deformation

21. The _____ of a quantity whose value decreases with time is the interval required for the quantity to decay to half of its initial value. The concept originated in describing how long it takes atoms to undergo radioactive decay but also applies in a wide variety of other situations.

The term '_____' dates to 1907.

a. 15 theorem
b. Half-life
c. BIBO stability
d. BDDC

22. _____ is the concept of adding accumulated interest back to the principal, so that interest is earned on interest from that moment on. The act of declaring interest to be principal is called compounding (i.e., interest is compounded.) A loan, for example, may have its interest compounded every month: in this case, a loan with $100 principal and 1% interest per month would have a balance of $101 at the end of the first month.

a. BDDC
b. 15 theorem
c. BIBO stability
d. Compound interest

23. The _____ of an object is the extra energy which it possesses due to its motion. It is defined as the work needed to accelerate a body of a given mass from rest to its current velocity. Having gained this energy during its acceleration, the body maintains this _____ unless its speed changes.

a. 15 theorem
b. BDDC
c. Kinetic energy
d. Potential energy

24. _____ is a PDE solver of Maxwell's equations based on the method of moments. It is a 3-D planar electromagnetic (EM) simulator used for passive circuit analysis. It is presently marketed by Agilent Technologies EEsof division, but the tool was original developed by a Belgian company, Alphabit, a spinoff from IMEC, which was acquired by Hewlett-Packard and later spun out as part of Agilent.

a. Partial Element Equivalent Circuit
b. Trefftz method
c. Momentum
d. Stencil

25. The _____ is a polynomial mapping of degree 2, often cited as an archetypal example of how complex, chaotic behaviour can arise from very simple non-linear dynamical equations. The map was popularized in a seminal 1976 paper by the biologist Robert May, in part as a discrete-time demographic model analogous to the logistic equation first created by Pierre François Verhulst. Mathematically, the _____ is written

$$(1) \quad x_{n+1} = rx_n(1 - x_n)$$

where:

x_n is a number between zero and one, and represents the population at year n, and hence x_0 represents the initial population (at year 0)

r is a positive number, and represents a combined rate for reproduction and starvation.

a. BIBO stability   b. Logistic map
c. 15 theorem   d. BDDC

26. The _____ are a pair of first order, non-linear, differential equations frequently used to describe the dynamics of biological systems in which two species interact, one a predator and one its prey. They were proposed independently by Alfred J. Lotka in 1925 and Vito Volterra in 1926.

where

- y is the number of some predator;
- x is the number of its prey;
- dy/dt and dx/dt represents the growth of the two populations against time;
- t represents the time; and
- >α, >β, >γ and >δ are parameters representing the interaction of the two species.

When multiplied out, the equations take a form useful for physical interpretation. Their origin should be considered from a more general framework,

where both functions represent per capita growth rates of the prey and predator, respectively.

a. BIBO stability   b. BDDC
c. 15 theorem   d. Lotka-Volterra equations

27. In mathematics, the point $\tilde{x} \in \mathbb{R}^n$ is an _____ for the differential equation

$$\frac{d\mathbf{x}}{dt} = \mathbf{f}(t, \mathbf{x})$$

if $\mathbf{f}(t, \tilde{\mathbf{x}}) = 0$ for all t.

Similarly, the point $\tilde{\mathbf{x}} \in \mathbb{R}^n$ is an _____ (or fixed point) for the difference equation

$$\mathbf{x}_{k+1} = \mathbf{f}(k, \mathbf{x}_k)$$

if $\mathbf{f}(k, \tilde{\mathbf{x}}) = \tilde{\mathbf{x}}$ for $k = 0, 1, 2, \ldots$.

Equilibria can be classified by looking at the signs of the eigenvalues of the linearization of the equations about the equilibria.

a. ALGOR
b. ACTRAN
c. AUSM
d. Equilibrium point

28. A _____ is a visual display of certain characteristics of certain kinds of differential equations.

Phase planes are useful in visualizing the behavior of physical systems; in particular, of oscillatory systems such as predator-prey models These models can 'spiral in' towards zero, 'spiral out' towards infinity, or reach neutrally stable situations called centres where the path traced out can be either circular, elliptical, or ovoid, or some variant thereof.

a. Separation of variables
b. Frobenius method
c. Power series method
d. Phase plane

29. A _____ is a geometric representation of the trajectories of a dynamical system in the phase plane. Each set of initial conditions is represented by a different curve, or point.

they are an invaluable tool in studying dynamical systems.

a. 15 theorem
b. BDDC
c. BIBO stability
d. Phase portrait

Chapter 8. Infinite Sequences and Series

1. In mathematics, _____, first defined by the mathematician Daniel Bernoulli and generalized by Friedrich Bessel, are canonical solutions y(x) of Bessel's differential equation:

$$x^2 \frac{d^2y}{dx^2} + x\frac{dy}{dx} + (x^2 - \alpha^2)y = 0$$

for an arbitrary real or complex number α (the order of the Bessel function.) The most common and important special case is where α is an integer n.

Although α and −α produce the same differential equation, it is conventional to define different _____ for these two orders (e.g., so that the _____ are mostly smooth functions of α.)

a. Bessel functions
b. Multiplication theorem
c. 15 theorem
d. Logarithmic integral function

2. In mathematics, a _____ is an ordered list of objects (or events). Like a set, it contains members (also called elements or terms), and the number of terms (possibly infinite) is called the length of the _____. Unlike a set, order matters, and the exact same elements can appear multiple times at different positions in the _____.

a. BDDC
b. Y-intercept
c. Sequence
d. 15 theorem

3. In vector calculus, the _____ is an operator that measures the magnitude of a vector field's source or sink at a given point; the _____ of a vector field is a (signed) scalar. For example, consider air as it is heated or cooled. The relevant vector field for this example is the velocity of the moving air at a point.

a. Triple product
b. Gradient theorem
c. Divergence Theorem
d. Divergence

4. In calculus, an _____ is the limit of a definite integral as an endpoint of the interval of integration approaches either a specified real number or ∞ or −∞ or, in some cases, as both endpoints approach limits.

Specifically, an _____ is a limit of the form

$$\lim_{b \to \infty} \int_a^b f(x)\,dx, \qquad \lim_{a \to -\infty} \int_a^b f(x)\,dx,$$

or of the form

$$\lim_{c \to b^-} \int_a^c f(x)\,dx, \qquad \lim_{c \to a^+} \int_c^b f(x)\,dx,$$

in which one takes a limit in one or the other (or sometimes both) endpoints. Improper integrals may also occur at an interior point of the domain of integration, or at multiple such points.

a. Improper integral   b. AUSM
c. ACTRAN   d. ALGOR

5. Integration is an important concept in mathematics, specifically in the field of calculus and, more broadly, mathematical analysis. Given a function f of a real variable x and an interval [a, b] of the real line, the _____

$$\int_a^b f(x)\,dx,$$

is defined informally to be the net signed area of the region in the xy-plane bounded by the graph of f, the x-axis, and the vertical lines x = a and x = b.

The term '_____' may also refer to the notion of antiderivative, a function F whose derivative is the given function f.

a. Indefinite integral   b. Integrand
c. Integral   d. Integral test for convergence

6. In mathematics, the concept of a '_____' is used to describe the behavior of a function as its argument or input either 'gets close' to some point, or as the argument becomes arbitrarily large; or the behavior of a sequence's elements as their index increases indefinitely. Limits are used in calculus and other branches of mathematical analysis to define derivatives and continuity.

In formulas, _____ is usually abbreviated as lim

a. BIBO stability   b. Limit
c. 15 theorem   d. BDDC

7. In calculus, the _____ is a theorem regarding the limit of a function.

The _____ is a technical result which is very important in proofs in calculus and mathematical analysis. It is typically used to confirm the limit of a function via comparison with two other functions whose limits are known or easily computed.

a. 15 theorem   b. Limit of a sequence
c. Table of limits   d. Squeeze Theorem

8. In mathematics, a _____ is a function which preserves the given order. This concept first arose in calculus, and was later generalized to the more abstract setting of order theory.

In calculus, a function f defined on a subset of the real numbers with real values is called monotonic (also monotonically increasing or non-decreasing), if for all x and y such that x >≤ y one has f(x) >≤ f(y), so f preserves the order.

a. Monotonic function
c. 15 theorem
b. Pseudo-differential operator
d. Pettis integral

9. In mathematics, a function f defined on some set X with real or complex values is a _____ function, if the set of its values is _____. In other words, there exists a number M>0 such that

$$|f(x)| \leq M$$

for all x in X.

Sometimes, if $f(x) \leq A$ for all x in X, then the function is said to be _____ above by A.

a. Differential calculus
c. Stationary phase approximation
b. Caccioppoli set
d. Bounded

10. _____ is a method of mathematical proof typically used to establish that a given statement is true of all natural numbers. It is done by proving that the first statement in the infinite sequence of statements is true, and then proving that if any one statement in the infinite sequence of statements is true, then so is the next one.

The method can be extended to prove statements about more general well-founded structures, such as trees; this generalization, known as structural induction, is used in mathematical logic and computer science.

a. BDDC
c. 15 theorem
b. BIBO stability
d. Mathematical induction

11. In mathematics, the _____ of two positive real numbers x and y is defined as follows:

First compute the arithmetic mean of x and y and call it a_1. Next compute the geometric mean of x and y and call it g_1; this is the square root of the product xy:

$$a_1 = \frac{x+y}{2}$$

$$g_1 = \sqrt{xy}.$$

Chapter 8. Infinite Sequences and Series

Then iterate this operation with a_1 taking the place of x and g_1 taking the place of y. In this way, two sequences (a_n) and (g_n) are defined:

$$a_{n+1} = \frac{a_n + g_n}{2}$$

$$g_{n+1} = \sqrt{a_n g_n}.$$

These two sequences converge to the same number, which is the _____ of x and y; it is denoted by M(x, y), or sometimes by agm(x, y.)

    a. ACTRAN   b. AUSM
    c. ALGOR   d. Arithmetic-geometric mean

12. In probability theory and statistics, the _____ (or expectation value or mean and for continuous random variables with a density function it is the probability density -weighted integral of the possible values.

The term '_____' can be misleading.

    a. AUSM   b. ACTRAN
    c. Expected value   d. ALGOR

13. Cantor defined two kinds of _____ numbers, the ordinal numbers and the cardinal numbers. Ordinal numbers may be identified with well-ordered sets, or counting carried on to any stopping point, including points after an _____ number have already been counted. Generalizing finite and the ordinary _____ sequences which are maps from the positive integers leads to mappings from ordinal numbers, and transfinite sequences.

    a. ALGOR   b. Infinite
    c. AUSM   d. ACTRAN

14. In mathematics, a _____ is an infinite series that is not convergent, meaning that the infinite sequence of the partial sums of the series does not have a limit.

If a series converges, the individual terms of the series must approach zero. Thus any series in which the individual terms do not approach zero diverges.

    a. BDDC   b. Divergent series
    c. 15 theorem   d. BIBO stability

15. Call S_N the _____ to N of the sequence {a_n}, or _____ of the series. A series is the sequence of partial sums, {S_N}.

When talking about series, one can refer either to the sequence {S_N} of the partial sums, or to the sum of the series,

$$\sum_{n=0}^{\infty} a_n$$

i.e., the limit of the sequence of partial sums - it is clear which one is meant from context.

a. Root test
b. Periodic function
c. Minimum
d. Partial sum

16. In mathematics, a _____ is a constant multiplicative factor of a certain object. For example, in the expression $9x^2$, the _____ of x^2 is 9.

The object can be such things as a variable, a vector, a function, etc.

a. Coefficient
b. Difference polynomial
c. Leading coefficient
d. Degree of the polynomial

17. In mathematics, a _____ is a series with a constant ratio between successive terms. For example, the series

$$\frac{1}{2} + \frac{1}{4} + \frac{1}{8} + \frac{1}{16} + \cdots$$

is geometric, because each term is equal to half of the previous term. The sum of this series is 1, as illustrated in the following picture:

_____ are one of the simplest examples of infinite series with finite sums.

a. Sequence transformation
b. Telescoping series
c. Geometric series
d. Converge absolutely

18. The terms of the series are often produced according to a certain rule, such as by a formula, by an algorithm, by a sequence of measurements, or even by a random number generator. As there are an infinite number of terms, this notion is often called an _____. Unlike finite summations, series need tools from mathematical analysis to be fully understood and manipulated.

a. Extreme value
b. Extreme Value Theorem
c. Integration by substitution
d. Infinite series

19. In acoustics and telecommunication, a _____ of a wave is a component frequency of the signal that is an integer multiple of the fundamental frequency. For example, if the fundamental frequency is f, the harmonics have frequencies f, 2f, 3f, 4f, etc. The harmonics have the property that they are all periodic at the fundamental frequency, therefore the sum of harmonics is also periodic at that frequency.

a. Harmonic
b. BIBO stability
c. 15 theorem
d. BDDC

20. In mathematics, the _____ is the infinite series

$$\sum_{k=1}^{\infty} \frac{1}{k} = 1 + \frac{1}{2} + \frac{1}{3} + \frac{1}{4} + \cdots.$$

Its name derives from the concept of overtones, or harmonics, in music: the wavelengths of the overtones of a vibrating string are 1/2, 1/3, 1/4, etc., of the string's fundamental wavelength. Every term of the series after the first is the harmonic mean of the neighboring terms; the term harmonic mean likewise derives from music.

The _____ diverges to infinity, albeit rather slowly (the first 10^{43} terms sum to less than 100 .)

a. BIBO stability
b. 15 theorem
c. BDDC
d. Harmonic series

21. In mathematics, a _____ is an informal expression referring to a series whose sum can be found by exploiting the circumstance that nearly every term cancels with either a succeeding or preceding term. Such a technique is also known as the method of differences.

For example, the series

$$\sum_{n=1}^{\infty} \frac{1}{n(n+1)}$$

simplifies as

$$\sum_{n=1}^{\infty} \frac{1}{n(n+1)} = \sum_{n=1}^{\infty} \left(\frac{1}{n} - \frac{1}{n+1} \right)$$
$$= \left(1 - \frac{1}{2} \right) + \left(\frac{1}{2} - \frac{1}{3} \right) + \cdots$$
$$= 1 + \left(-\frac{1}{2} + \frac{1}{2} \right) + \left(-\frac{1}{3} + \frac{1}{3} \right) + \cdots = 1.$$

Chapter 8. Infinite Sequences and Series

Although telescoping can be a useful technique, there are pitfalls to watch out for:

$$0 = \sum_{n=1}^{\infty} 0 = \sum_{n=1}^{\infty}(1-1) = 1 + \sum_{n=1}^{\infty}(-1+1) = 1$$

is not correct because regrouping of terms is invalid unless the individual terms converge to 0; see Grandi's series.

a. Telescoping series
b. Sequence transformation
c. Converge absolutely
d. Geometric series

22. In mathematics, the nth term _____ is a simple test for the divergence of an infinite series:

- If $\lim_{n \to \infty} a_n \neq 0$ or if the limit does not exist, then $\sum_{n=1}^{\infty} a_n$ diverges.

Many authors do not name this test or give it a shorter name.

Unlike stronger convergence tests, the term test cannot prove by itself that a series converges. In particular, the converse to the test is not true; instead all one can say is:

- If $\lim_{n \to \infty} a_n = 0$, then $\sum_{n=1}^{\infty} a_n$ may or may not converge. In other words, if $\lim_{n \to \infty} a_n = 0$, the test is inconclusive.

The harmonic series is a classic example of a divergent series whose terms limit to zero. The more general class of p-series,

$$\sum_{n=1}^{\infty} \frac{1}{n^p},$$

exemplifies the possible results of the test:

- If p ≤ 0, then the term test identifies the series as divergent.
- If 0 < p ≤ 1, then the term test is inconclusive, but the series is divergent by the integral test for convergence.
- If 1 < p, then the term test is inconclusive, but the series is convergent, again by the integral test for convergence.

The test is typically proved in contrapositive form:

- If $\sum_{n=1}^{\infty} a_n$ converges, then $\lim_{n \to \infty} a_n = 0$.

If s_n are the partial sums of the series, then the assumption that the series converges means that

$$\lim_{n \to \infty} s_n = s$$

for some number s. Then

$$\lim_{n \to \infty} a_n = \lim_{n \to \infty} (s_n - s_{n-1}) = s - s = 0.$$

The assumption that the series converges means that it passes Cauchy's convergence test: for every $\varepsilon > 0$ there is a number N such that

$$|a_{n+1} + a_{n+2} + \ldots + a_{n+p}| < \varepsilon$$

holds for all n > N and p ≥ 1. Setting p = 1 recovers the definition of the statement

$$\lim_{n \to \infty} a_n = 0.$$

The simplest version of the term test applies to infinite series of real numbers.

a. First derivative test
b. Test for Divergence
c. Nth term
d. Visual Calculus

23. In mathematics, the _____, introduced by German mathematician Georg Cantor in 1883 (but discovered in 1875 by Henry John Stephen Smith), is a set of points lying on a single line segment that has a number of remarkable and deep properties. Through consideration of it, Cantor and others helped lay the foundations of modern general topology. Although Cantor himself defined the set in a general, abstract way, the most common modern construction is the Cantor ternary set, built by removing the middle thirds of a line segment.
   a. 15 theorem
   b. BDDC
   c. Planar Lamina
   d. Cantor set

24. The _____ is a plane fractal first described by Waclaw Sierpinski in 1916. The carpet is a generalization of the Cantor set to two dimensions (another is Cantor dust.) Sierpinski demonstrated that this fractal is a universal curve, in that any possible one-dimensional graph, projected onto the two-dimensional plane, is homeomorphic to a subset of the _____.

Chapter 8. Infinite Sequences and Series

a. BDDC
c. Siegel disc
b. 15 theorem
d. Sierpinski carpet

25. In mathematics, an _____ is an infinite series of the form

$$\sum_{n=0}^{\infty}(-1)^n a_n,$$

with $a_n \geq 0$ (or $a_n \leq 0$) for all n. A finite sum of this kind is an alternating sum. An _____ converges if the terms a_n converge to 0 monotonically.

a. Alternating Series
c. Uniform convergence
b. Infinite series
d. Extreme value

26. The _____ converges:

$$\sum_{k=1}^{\infty}\frac{(-1)^{k+1}}{k} = 1 - \frac{1}{2} + \frac{1}{3} - \frac{1}{4} + \cdots = \ln 2 = 0.693\,147\,180\,\ldots.$$

This equality is a consequence of the Mercator series, the Taylor series for the natural logarithm. Another equality, similar in form to Mercator's series, is:

$$\sum_{k=0}^{\infty}\frac{(-1)^k}{2k+1} = 1 - \frac{1}{3} + \frac{1}{5} - \frac{1}{7} + \cdots = \arctan(1) = \frac{\pi}{4}.$$

This is a consequence of the Taylor series representation of the inverse tangent function (which has a radius of convergence of 1.)

The nth partial sum of the diverging harmonic series,

$$H_n = \sum_{k=1}^{n}\frac{1}{k},$$

is called the nth harmonic number.

a. ACTRAN
c. AUSM
b. ALGOR
d. Alternating harmonic series

27. A _____ is an expression which compares quantities relative to each other. The most common examples involve two quantities, but in theory any number of quantities can be compared. In mathematical terms, they are represented by separating each quantity with a colon, for example the _____ 2:3, which is read as the _____ 'two to three'.

a. Ratio
b. Sequence
c. 15 theorem
d. BDDC

28. In mathematics, a _____ (in one variable) is an infinite series of the form

$$f(x) = \sum_{n=0}^{\infty} a_n (x-c)^n = a_0 + a_1(x-c)^1 + a_2(x-c)^2 + a_3(x-c)^3 + \cdots$$

where a_n represents the coefficient of the nth term, c is a constant, and x varies around c (for this reason one sometimes speaks of the series as being centered at c

In many situations c is equal to zero, for instance when considering a Maclaurin series.

a. Power series
b. Differential calculus
c. Mountain pass theorem
d. Caccioppoli set

29. In mathematics, the _____ of a power series is a non-negative quantity, either a real number or ∞ that represents a domain (within the radius) in which the series will converge. Within the _____, a power series converges absolutely and uniformly on compacta as well. If the series converges, it is the Taylor series of the analytic function to which it converges inside its _____.

a. Motor variable
b. Movable singularity
c. Radius of convergence
d. Principal values

30. In calculus, a branch of mathematics, the _____ is a measurement of how a function changes when its input changes. Loosely speaking, a _____ can be thought of as how much a quantity is changing at some given point. For example, the _____ of the position (or distance) of a vehicle with respect to time is the instantaneous velocity (respectively, instantaneous speed) at which the vehicle is traveling.

The process of finding a _____ is called differentiation. The fundamental theorem of calculus states that differentiation is the reverse process to integration.

a. Mountain pass theorem
b. Derivative
c. Concave upwards
d. Ramp function

31. In mathematics, the _____ is a representation of a function as an infinite sum of terms calculated from the values of its derivatives at a single point. It may be regarded as the limit of the Taylor polynomials. If the series is centered at zero, the series is also called a Maclaurin series.

a. Taylor series
b. BDDC
c. 15 theorem
d. BIBO stability

32. The _____ is a function in mathematics. The application of this function to a value x is written as exp(x). Equivalently, this can be written in the form e^x, where e is a mathematical constant, the base of the natural logarithm, which equals approximately 2.718281828, and is also known as Euler's number.

a. Integral part
b. ACTRAN
c. Area hyperbolic functions
d. Exponential function

33. A surface normal to a flat surface is a vector which is perpendicular to that surface. A normal to a non-flat surface at a point P on the surface is a vector perpendicular to the tangent plane to that surface at P. The word 'normal' is also used as an adjective: a line normal to a plane, the normal component of a force, the _____, etc. The concept of normality generalizes to orthogonality.
   a. Hyperbolic paraboloid
   b. Paraboloid
   c. Normal vector
   d. PDE surfaces

34. In calculus, _____ gives a sequence of approximations of a differentiable function around a given point by polynomials (the Taylor polynomials of that function) whose coefficients depend only on the derivatives of the function at that point. The theorem also gives precise estimates on the size of the error in the approximation. The theorem is named after the mathematician Brook Taylor, who stated it in 1712, though the result was first discovered 41 years earlier in 1671 by James Gregory.
   a. Complex analysis
   b. Leibniz differential
   c. Taylor's theorem
   d. Continuous function

35. In elementary algebra, a _____ is a polynomial with two terms--the sum of two monomials--often bound by parenthesis or brackets when operated upon. It is the simplest kind of polynomial other than monomials.

   - The _____ $a^2 - b^2$ can be factored as the product of two other binomials:

     $a^2 - b^2 = (a + b)(a - b.)$

     $$a^{n+1} - b^{n+1} = (a - b) \sum_{k=0}^{n} a^k b^{n-k}$$

     This is a special case of the more general formula:

   - The product of a pair of linear binomials $(ax + b)$ and $(cx + d)$ is:

     $(ax + b)(cx + d) = acx^2 + axd + bcx + bd.$

   - A _____ raised to the nth power, represented as

     $(a + b)^n$

     can be expanded by means of the _____ theorem or, equivalently, using Pascal's triangle. Taking a simple example, the perfect square _____ $(p + q)^2$ can be found by squaring the :first digit, adding twice the product of the first and second digit and finally adding the square of the second digit, to give $p^2 + 2pq + q^2$.

   a. Multinomial theorem
   b. Partial fractions
   c. Completing the square
   d. Binomial

36. In mathematics, the _____ is an important formula giving the expansion of powers of sums. Its simplest version states that

$$(x+y)^n = \sum_{k=0}^{n} \binom{n}{k} x^{n-k} y^k \qquad (1)$$

for any real or complex numbers x and y, and any non-negative integer n. The binomial coefficient appearing in (1) may be defined in terms of the factorial function n!:

$$\binom{n}{k} = \frac{n!}{k!\,(n-k)!}.$$

For example, here are the cases where 2 ≤ n ≤ 5:

$$(x+y)^2 = x^2 + 2xy + y^2$$
$$(x+y)^3 = x^3 + 3x^2y + 3xy^2 + y^3$$
$$(x+y)^4 = x^4 + 4x^3y + 6x^2y^2 + 4xy^3 + y^4$$
$$(x+y)^5 = x^5 + 5x^4y + 10x^3y^2 + 10x^2y^3 + 5xy^4 + y^5.$$

Formula (1) is valid more generally for any elements x and y of a semiring as long as xy = yx.

  a. Binomial Theorem
  c. Lah numbers
  b. Trinomial expansion
  d. Stirling transform

37. In mathematics, the _____ generalizes the purely algebraic formula of the binomial theorem to complex values of α. It is also a special case of a Newton series. The _____ is the series

$$(1+x)^\alpha = \sum_{k=0}^{\infty} \binom{\alpha}{k} x^k = \sum_{k=0}^{\infty} \frac{\prod_{a=0}^{k-1}(\alpha - a)\, x^k}{k!}$$

where α is a complex number and

$$\binom{\alpha}{k} = \frac{\alpha(\alpha-1)(\alpha-2)\cdots(\alpha-k+1)}{k!}$$

is the (generalized) binomial coefficient (if α is a non negative integer, then the (α + 1) th term and all later terms in the series are zero, since each one contains a factor equal to (α − α): thus, in that case, the summation reduces to the algebraic binomial formula.)

a. Leibniz formula
b. Taylor's theorem
c. Fundamental Theorem of Calculus
d. Binomial series

38. The _____ in some data is the discrepancy between an exact value and some approximation to it. An _____ can occur because

1. the measurement of the data is not precise (due to the instruments), or
2. approximations are used instead of the real data (e.g., 3.14 instead of π.)

In the mathematical field of numerical analysis, the numerical stability of an algorithm in numerical analysis indicates how the error is propagated by the algorithm.

One commonly distinguishes between the relative error and the absolute error. The absolute error is the magnitude of the difference between the exact value and the approximation.

a. ALGOR
b. AUSM
c. Approximation Error
d. ACTRAN

39. In infinitesimal calculus, a _____ is traditionally an infinitesimally small change in a variable. For example, if x is a variable, then a change in the value of x is often denoted Δx (or δx when this change is considered to be small.) The _____ dx represents such a change, but is infinitely small.

a. Related rates
b. Differential
c. Dirichlet integral
d. Continuous function

40. A _____ is a mathematical equation for an unknown function of one or several variables that relates the values of the function itself and of its derivatives of various orders. they play a prominent role in engineering, physics, economics and other disciplines.

A simplified real world example of a _____ is modeling the acceleration of a ball falling through the air (considering only gravity and air resistance.)

a. Petrovsky lacuna
b. Differential equation
c. Structural stability
d. Lax pair

41. In mathematics, a (topological) _____ is defined as follows: let I be an interval of real numbers (i.e. a non-empty connected subset of $\mathbb{R}$); then a _____ γ is a continuous mapping $\gamma : I \to X$, where X is a topological space. The _____ γ is said to be simple if it is injective, i.e. if for all x, y in I, we have $\gamma(x) = \gamma(y) \implies x = y$. If I is a closed bounded interval $[a, b]$, we also allow the possibility $\gamma(a) = \gamma(b)$ (this convention makes it possible to talk about closed simple _____.)

a. Closed curve
b. Tractrix
c. Prolate cycloid
d. Curve

Chapter 9. Vectors and the Geometry of Space

1. In mathematics and its applications, a _____ system is a system for assigning an n-tuple of numbers or scalars to each point in an n-dimensional space. This concept is part of the theory of manifolds. 'Scalars' in many cases means real numbers, but, depending on context, can mean complex numbers or elements of some other commutative ring.

   a. Coordinate
   b. 15 theorem
   c. Cylindrical coordinate system
   d. Spherical coordinate system

2. In mathematics, the _____ is used to determine each point uniquely in a plane through two numbers, usually called the x-coordinate or abscissa and the y-coordinate or ordinate of the point. To define the coordinates, two perpendicular directed lines, are specified, as well as the unit length, which is marked off on the two axes Cartesian coordinate systems are also used in space and in higher dimensions.

   a. Spherical coordinate system
   b. 15 theorem
   c. Coordinate
   d. Cartesian coordinate system

3. In mathematics, _____ and minima, known collectively as extrema, are the largest value (maximum) or smallest value (minimum), that a function takes in a point either within a given neighbourhood (local extremum) or on the function domain in its entirety (global extremum.)

   Throughout, a point refers to an input (x), while a value refers to an output (y): one distinguishing between the maximum value and the point (or points) at which it occurs.

   A real-valued function f defined on the real line is said to have a local maximum point at the point x^*, if there exists some $\varepsilon > 0$, such that $f(x^*) \geq f(x)$ when $|x - x^*| < \varepsilon$.

   a. Standard part function
   b. Fundamental Theorem of Calculus
   c. Partial sum
   d. Maxima

4. The _____ are a pair of first order, non-linear, differential equations frequently used to describe the dynamics of biological systems in which two species interact, one a predator and one its prey. They were proposed independently by Alfred J. Lotka in 1925 and Vito Volterra in 1926.

   where

   - y is the number of some predator;
   - x is the number of its prey;
   - dy/dt and dx/dt represents the growth of the two populations against time;
   - t represents the time; and
   - >α, >β, >γ and >δ are parameters representing the interaction of the two species.

When multiplied out, the equations take a form useful for physical interpretation. Their origin should be considered from a more general framework,

where both functions represent per capita growth rates of the prey and predator, respectively.

    a. Lotka-Volterra equations   b. BIBO stability
    c. 15 theorem   d. BDDC

5. A _____ is perfectly round geometrical object in three-dimensional space, such as the shape of a round ball. Like a circle in two dimensions, a perfect _____ is completely symmetrical around its center, with all points on the surface lying the same distance r from the center point. This distance r is known as the radius of the _____.
    a. Tortuosity   b. Differentiable manifold
    c. Sphere   d. Minimal surface

6. A _____ is a reference from which measurements are made. In surveying and geodesy, a datum is a set of reference points on the earth's surface against which position measurements are made, and (often) an associated model of the shape of the earth (reference ellipsoid) to define a geographic coordinate system. Horizontal datums are used for describing a point on the earth's surface, in latitude and longitude or another coordinate system.
    a. BIBO stability   b. Geodetic datum
    c. 15 theorem   d. BDDC

7. In linear algebra, the null vector or _____ is the vector (0, 0, â€¦, 0) in Euclidean space, all of whose components are zero. It is usually written $\vec{0}$ or 0 or simply 0. A _____ has no direction.
    a. Dot product   b. Direction vector
    c. Scalar multiplication   d. Zero Vector

8. In mathematics, the _____ of two monic polynomials P and Q over a field k is defined as the product

$$\mathrm{res}(P,Q) = \prod_{(x,y):\, P(x)=0,\, Q(y)=0} (x-y),$$

of the differences of their roots, where x and y take on values in the algebraic closure of k. For non-monic polynomials with leading coefficients p and q, respectively, the above product is multiplied by

$$p^{\deg Q} q^{\deg P}.$$

- The _____ is the determinant of the Sylvester matrix (and of the Bezout matrix.)

- When Q is separable, the above product can be rewritten to

$$\operatorname{res}(P, Q) = \prod_{P(x)=0} Q(x)$$

and this expression remains unchanged if Q is reduced modulo P. Note that, when non-monic, this includes the factor $q^{\deg P}$ but still needs the factor $p^{\deg Q}$.

- Let $P' = P \mod Q$. The above idea can be continued by swapping the roles of P' and Q. However, P' has a set of roots different from that of P. This can be resolved by writing $\prod_{Q(y)=0} P'(y)$ as a determinant again, where P' has leading zero coefficients. This determinant can now be simplified by iterative expansion with respect to the column, where only the leading coefficient q of Q appears.

$$\operatorname{res}(P, Q) = q^{\deg P - \deg P'} \cdot \operatorname{res}(P', Q)$$

Continuing this procedure ends up in a variant of the Euclidean algorithm. This procedure needs quadratic runtime.

a. Coefficient
c. Leading coefficient
b. Difference polynomial
d. Resultant

9. A _____, $F_{net} = F_1 + F_2 + â€¦$ (also known as a resultant force) is a vector produced when two or more forces { F_1, F_2, â€¦ } act upon a single object. It is calculated by vector addition of the force vectors acting upon the object. A _____ can also be defined as the overall force acting on an object, when all the individual forces acting on the object are added together.

a. BIBO stability
c. 15 theorem
b. BDDC
d. Net force

10. In mathematics, a _____ in a normed vector space is a vector (often a spatial vector) whose length is 1 (the unit length.) A _____ is often denoted by a lowercase letter with a superscribed caret or e;hate;, like this: $\hat{\imath}$.

In Euclidean space, the dot product of two unit vectors is simply the cosine of the angle between them.

a. Unit vector
b. ACTRAN
c. Overdetermined
d. ALGOR

11. In mathematics, the _____ is an operation which takes two vectors over the real numbers R and returns a real-valued scalar quantity. It is the standard inner product of the orthonormal Euclidean space. It contrasts with the cross product which produces a vector result.
    a. Vector-valued function
    b. Homogeneous function
    c. Dot product
    d. Direction vector

12. In mathematics, two vectors are _____ if they are perpendicular, i.e., they form a right angle. For example, a subway and the street above, although they do not physically intersect, are _____ if they cross at a right angle.
    a. ACTRAN
    b. ALGOR
    c. AUSM
    d. Orthogonal

13. In mathematics, an _____ is an infinite series of the form

$$\sum_{n=0}^{\infty}(-1)^n a_n,$$

with $a_n \geq 0$ (or $a_n \leq 0$) for all n. A finite sum of this kind is an alternating sum. An _____ converges if the terms a_n converge to 0 monotonically.

   a. Alternating Series
   b. Uniform convergence
   c. Extreme value
   d. Infinite series

14. _____ is the tendency of a force to rotate an object about an axis (or fulcrum or pivot.) Just as a force is a push or a pull, a _____ can be thought of as a twist. The symbol for _____ is τ, the Greek letter tau.
    a. BIBO stability
    b. BDDC
    c. Torque
    d. 15 theorem

15. In geometry, a _____ is a three-dimensional figure formed by six parallelograms. It is to a parallelogram as a cube is to a square: Euclidean geometry supports all four notions but affine geometry admits only parallelograms and parallelepipeds. Three equivalent definitions of _____ are

   - a polyhedron with six faces (hexahedron), each of which is a parallelogram,
   - a hexahedron with three pairs of parallel faces, and
   - a prism of which the base is a parallelogram.

The cuboid (six rectangular faces), cube (six square faces), and the rhombohedron (six rhombus faces) are all specific cases of _____.

Parallelepipeds are a subclass of the prismatoids.

a. BDDC
b. BIBO stability
c. 15 theorem
d. Parallelepiped

16. In vector calculus, there are two ways of multiplying three vectors together, to make a _____ of vectors. Three vectors defining a parallelepiped

The scalar _____ is defined as the dot product of one of the vectors with the cross product of the other two.

Geometrically, the scalar _____

$$\mathbf{a} \cdot (\mathbf{b} \times \mathbf{c})$$

is the (signed) volume of the parallelepiped defined by the three vectors given.

a. Divergence Theorem
b. Divergence
c. Gradient theorem
d. Triple product

17. In mathematics, _____ are a method of defining a curve. A simple kinematical example is when one uses a time parameter to determine the position, velocity, and other information about a body in motion.

Abstractly, a relation is given in the form of an equation, and it is shown also to be the image of functions from items such as R^n.

a. Multivariable calculus
b. Parametric equations
c. Differential operator
d. Laplace operator

18. A surface normal to a flat surface is a vector which is perpendicular to that surface. A normal to a non-flat surface at a point P on the surface is a vector perpendicular to the tangent plane to that surface at P. The word 'normal' is also used as an adjective: a line normal to a plane, the normal component of a force, the _____, etc. The concept of normality generalizes to orthogonality.

a. Normal vector
b. Paraboloid
c. Hyperbolic paraboloid
d. PDE surfaces

19. A _____ is an algebraic equation in which each term is either a constant or the product of a constant and (the first power of) a single variable. Linear equations can have one, two, three or more variables. Linear equations occur with great regularity in applied mathematics.

a. BDDC
b. Cubic function
c. 15 theorem
d. Linear equation

20. _____ is a term in geometry and in everyday life that refers to a property in Euclidean space of two or more lines or planes, or a combination of these. The existence and properties of parallel lines are the basis of Euclid's parallel postulate. Two lines parallel would be denoted as ABC DEF.

a. 15 theorem
b. BIBO stability
c. BDDC
d. Parallelism

21. In economics, the _____ functional form of production functions is widely used to represent the relationship of an output to inputs. It was proposed by Knut Wicksell (1851-1926), and tested against statistical evidence by Charles Cobb and Paul Douglas in 1900-1928.

For production, the function is

$$Y = AL^{\alpha}K^{\beta},$$

where:

- Y = total production (the monetary value of all goods produced in a year)
- L = labor input
- K = capital input
- A = total factor productivity
- α and β are the output elasticities of labor and capital, respectively. These values are constants determined by available technology.

Output elasticity measures the responsiveness of output to a change in levels of either labor or capital used in production, ceteris paribus. For example if α = 0.15, a 1% increase in labor would lead to approximately a 0.15% increase in output.

a. BIBO stability
b. BDDC
c. 15 theorem
d. Cobb-Douglas

22. The terms '_____' and 'independent variable' are used in similar but subtly different ways in mathematics and statistics as part of the standard terminology in those subjects. They are used to distinguish between two types of quantities being considered, separating them into those available at the start of a process and those being created by it, where the latter (dependent variables) are dependent on the former (independent variables.)

In traditional calculus, a function is defined as a relation between two terms called variables because their values vary.

a. Dependent variable
b. BIBO stability
c. 15 theorem
d. BDDC

23. In mathematics, the _____ (or replacement set) of a given function is the set of 'input' values for which the function is defined. For instance, the _____ of cosine would be all real numbers, while the _____ of the square root would be only numbers greater than or equal to 0 (ignoring complex numbers in both cases.) In a representation of a function in a xy Cartesian coordinate system, the _____ is represented on the x axis (or abscissa.)

a. BDDC
b. Domain
c. BIBO stability
d. 15 theorem

24. The terms 'dependent variable' and '_____' are used in similar but subtly different ways in mathematics and statistics as part of the standard terminology in those subjects. They are used to distinguish between two types of quantities being considered, separating them into those available at the start of a process and those being created by it, where the latter (dependent variables) are dependent on the former (independent variables.)

In traditional calculus, a function is defined as a relation between two terms called variables because their values vary.

   a. ALGOR   b. AUSM
   c. ACTRAN   d. Independent variable

25. In mathematics, the _____ of a function is the set of all 'output' values produced by that function. Sometimes it is called the image, or more precisely, the image of the domain of the function. If a function is a surjection then its _____ is equal to its codomain.

   a. Surjective   b. Range
   c. Piecewise-defined function   d. Constant function

26. In geometry, a _____ is a special plane curve generated by the trace of a fixed point on a small circle that rolls within a larger circle. It is comparable to the cycloid but instead of the circle rolling along a line, it rolls within a circle. The red curve is a _____ traced as the smaller black circle rolls around inside the larger blue circle (parameters are R=3.0, r=1.0, and so k=3), giving a deltoid.

If the smaller circle has radius r, and the larger circle has radius R = kr, then the parametric equations for the curve can be given by either:

$$x(\theta) = (R-r)\cos\theta + r\cos\left(\frac{R-r}{r}\theta\right)$$
$$y(\theta) = (R-r)\sin\theta - r\sin\left(\frac{R-r}{r}\theta\right),$$

or:

$$x(\theta) = r(k-1)\cos\theta + r\cos((k-1)\theta)$$
$$y(\theta) = r(k-1)\sin\theta - r\sin((k-1)\theta).$$

If k is an integer, then the curve is closed, and has k cusps (i.e., sharp corners, where the curve is not differentiable.)

   a. Kappa curve   b. Closed curve
   c. Bullet-nose curve   d. Hypocycloid

27. A _____ is one of the most curvilinear basic geometric shapes: It has two faces, zero vertices, and zero edges. The surface formed by the points at a fixed distance from a given straight line, the axis of the _____. The solid enclosed by this surface and by two planes perpendicular to the axis is also called a _____.

a. Right circular cylinder
b. BDDC
c. 15 theorem
d. Cylinder

28. The _____ is a doubly ruled surface shaped like a saddle. In a suitable coordinate system, it can be represented by the equation

$$z = \frac{x^2}{a^2} - \frac{y^2}{b^2}.$$

This is a _____ that opens up along the x-axis and down along the y-axis.

Paraboloid of revolution

With a = b an elliptic paraboloid is a paraboloid of revolution: a surface obtained by revolving a parabola around its axis.

a. PDE surfaces
b. Hyperbolic paraboloid
c. Parametric surface
d. Prolate

29. In mathematics, a _____ is a quadric surface of special kind. There are two kinds of paraboloids: elliptic and hyperbolic. The elliptic _____ is shaped like an oval cup and can have a maximum or minimum point.

a. Parametric surface
b. Normal vector
c. Normal line
d. Paraboloid

30. An _____ is a type of quadric surface that is a higher dimensional analogue of an ellipse. The equation of a standard axis-aligned _____ body in an xyz-Cartesian coordinate system is

$$\frac{x^2}{a^2} + \frac{y^2}{b^2} + \frac{z^2}{c^2} = 1$$

where a and b are the equatorial radii (along the x and y axes) and c is the polar radius (along the z-axis), all of which are fixed positive real numbers determining the shape of the _____.

More generally, a not-necessarily-axis-aligned _____ is defined by the equation

$$\mathbf{x}^T A \mathbf{x} = 1$$

where A is a symmetric positive definite matrix and x is a vector.

a. AUSM
b. Ellipsoid
c. ACTRAN
d. ALGOR

31. In geometry, an _____ is a plane curve produced by tracing the path of a chosen point of a circle -- called epicycle -- which rolls without slipping around a fixed circle. It is a particular kind of roulette.

If the smaller circle has radius r, and the larger circle has radius R = kr, then the parametric equations for the curve can be given by either:

$$x(\theta) = (R+r)\cos\theta - r\cos\left(\frac{R+r}{r}\theta\right)$$
$$y(\theta) = (R+r)\sin\theta - r\sin\left(\frac{R+r}{r}\theta\right),$$

or:

$$x(\theta) = r(k+1)\cos\theta - r\cos((k+1)\theta)$$
$$y(\theta) = r(k+1)\sin\theta - r\sin((k+1)\theta).$$

If k is an integer, then the curve is closed, and has k cusps (i.e., sharp corners, where the curve is not differentiable.)

a. ACTRAN
b. Asymptotic curve
c. Epicycloid
d. ALGOR

Chapter 10. Vector Functions

1. Cantor defined two kinds of _____ numbers, the ordinal numbers and the cardinal numbers. Ordinal numbers may be identified with well-ordered sets, or counting carried on to any stopping point, including points after an _____ number have already been counted. Generalizing finite and the ordinary _____ sequences which are maps from the positive integers leads to mappings from ordinal numbers, and transfinite sequences.

   a. AUSM
   b. ACTRAN
   c. ALGOR
   d. Infinite

2. In mathematics, the concept of a '_____' is used to describe the behavior of a function as its argument or input either 'gets close' to some point, or as the argument becomes arbitrarily large; or the behavior of a sequence's elements as their index increases indefinitely. Limits are used in calculus and other branches of mathematical analysis to define derivatives and continuity.

   In formulas, _____ is usually abbreviated as lim

   a. BDDC
   b. Limit
   c. BIBO stability
   d. 15 theorem

3. In mathematical optimization, the method of Lagrange multipliers provides a strategy for finding the maximum/minimum of a function subject to constraints.

   For example, consider the optimization problem

   $$\text{maximize } f(x,y)$$
   $$\text{subject to } g(x,y) = c.$$

   We introduce a new variable (λ) called a _____, and study the Lagrange function defined by

   $$\Lambda(x, y, \lambda) = f(x,y) - \lambda\Big(g(x,y) - c\Big).$$

   If (x,y)‰ is a maximum for the original constrained problem, then there exists a λ such that (x,y,λ)‰ is a stationary point for the Lagrange function (stationary points are those points where the partial derivatives of Λ are zero.) However, not all stationary points yield a solution of the original problem.

   a. BIBO stability
   b. BDDC
   c. 15 theorem
   d. Lagrange multiplier

4. A plane curve is a curve for which X is the Euclidean plane -- these are the examples first encountered -- or in some cases the projective plane. A _____ is a curve for which X is of three dimensions, usually Euclidean space; a skew curve is a _____ which lies in no plane. These definitions also apply to algebraic curves

   a. Space curve
   b. Folium of Descartes
   c. Hypocycloid
   d. Curtate cycloid

Chapter 10. Vector Functions

5. A _____ is a mathematical function that maps real numbers to vectors. Vector-valued functions can be defined as:

- $\mathbf{r}(t) = f(t)\hat{\mathbf{i}} + g(t)\hat{\mathbf{j}}$ or
- $\mathbf{r}(t) = f(t)\hat{\mathbf{i}} + g(t)\hat{\mathbf{j}} + h(t)\hat{\mathbf{k}}$

where f(t), g(t) and h(t) are the coordinate functions of the parameter t, and $\hat{\mathbf{i}}$, $\hat{\mathbf{j}}$, and $\hat{\mathbf{k}}$ are unit vectors. r(t) is a vector which has its tail at the origin and its head at the coordinates evaluated by the function.

The vector shown in the graph to the right is the evaluation of the function near t=19.5 (between 6π and 6.5π; i.e., somewhat more than 3 rotations.)

- a. Zero vector
- b. Direction vector
- c. Dot product
- d. Vector-valued function

6. In mathematics, a (topological) _____ is defined as follows: let I be an interval of real numbers (i.e. a non-empty connected subset of $\mathbb{R}$); then a _____ γ is a continuous mapping $\gamma : I \to X$, where X is a topological space. The _____ γ is said to be simple if it is injective, i.e. if for all x, y in I, we have $\gamma(x) = \gamma(y) \implies x = y$. If I is a closed bounded interval $[a, b]$, we also allow the possibility $\gamma(a) = \gamma(b)$ (this convention makes it possible to talk about closed simple _____.)

- a. Curve
- b. Tractrix
- c. Closed curve
- d. Prolate cycloid

7. In economics, the _____ functional form of production functions is widely used to represent the relationship of an output to inputs. It was proposed by Knut Wicksell (1851-1926), and tested against statistical evidence by Charles Cobb and Paul Douglas in 1900-1928.

For production, the function is

$$Y = AL^{\alpha}K^{\beta},$$

where:

- Y = total production (the monetary value of all goods produced in a year)
- L = labor input
- K = capital input
- A = total factor productivity
- α and β are the output elasticities of labor and capital, respectively. These values are constants determined by available technology.

Output elasticity measures the responsiveness of output to a change in levels of either labor or capital used in production, ceteris paribus. For example if α = 0.15, a 1% increase in labor would lead to approximately a 0.15% increase in output.

Chapter 10. Vector Functions

a. BDDC
b. BIBO stability
c. 15 theorem
d. Cobb-Douglas

8. The _____ are a pair of first order, non-linear, differential equations frequently used to describe the dynamics of biological systems in which two species interact, one a predator and one its prey. They were proposed independently by Alfred J. Lotka in 1925 and Vito Volterra in 1926.

where

- y is the number of some predator;
- x is the number of its prey;
- dy/dt and dx/dt represents the growth of the two populations against time;
- t represents the time; and
- >α, >β, >γ and >δ are parameters representing the interaction of the two species.

When multiplied out, the equations take a form useful for physical interpretation. Their origin should be considered from a more general framework,

where both functions represent per capita growth rates of the prey and predator, respectively.

a. BIBO stability
b. Lotka-Volterra equations
c. 15 theorem
d. BDDC

9. In mathematics, _____ are a method of defining a curve. A simple kinematical example is when one uses a time parameter to determine the position, velocity, and other information about a body in motion.

Abstractly, a relation is given in the form of an equation, and it is shown also to be the image of functions from items such as R^n.

a. Parametric equations
b. Laplace operator
c. Multivariable calculus
d. Differential operator

10. A _____ is a special kind of space curve, i.e. a smooth curve in three-space. As a mental image of a _____ one may take the spring (although the spring is not a curve, and so is technically not a _____, it does give a convenient mental picture.) A _____ is characterised by the fact that the tangent line at any point makes a constant angle with a fixed line.

- a. Helix
- b. 15 theorem
- c. BDDC
- d. BIBO stability

11. In calculus, a branch of mathematics, the _____ is a measurement of how a function changes when its input changes. Loosely speaking, a _____ can be thought of as how much a quantity is changing at some given point. For example, the _____ of the position (or distance) of a vehicle with respect to time is the instantaneous velocity (respectively, instantaneous speed) at which the vehicle is traveling.

The process of finding a _____ is called differentiation. The fundamental theorem of calculus states that differentiation is the reverse process to integration.

- a. Mountain pass theorem
- b. Ramp function
- c. Concave upwards
- d. Derivative

12. In mathematics, an _____ is a generalization for the concept of a function in which the dependent variable has not been given 'explicitly' in terms of the independent variable. To give a function f explicitly is to provide a prescription for determining the output value of the function y in terms of the input value x:

$$y = f(x.)$$

By contrast, the function is implicit if the value of y is obtained from x by solving an equation of the form:

$$R(x,y) = 0.$$

- a. Implicit differentiation
- b. Implicit function
- c. Automatic differentiation
- d. Ordinary differential equation

13. Integration is an important concept in mathematics, specifically in the field of calculus and, more broadly, mathematical analysis. Given a function f of a real variable x and an interval [a, b] of the real line, the _____

$$\int_a^b f(x)\,dx,$$

is defined informally to be the net signed area of the region in the xy-plane bounded by the graph of f, the x-axis, and the vertical lines x = a and x = b.

The term '_____' may also refer to the notion of antiderivative, a function F whose derivative is the given function f.

a. Integral	b. Integral test for convergence
c. Indefinite integral	d. Integrand

14. In geometry, the _____ (or simply the tangent) to a curve at a given point is the straight line that 'just touches' the curve at that point (in the sense explained more precisely below.) As it passes through the point of tangency, the _____ is 'going in the same direction' as the curve, and in this sense it is the best straight-line approximation to the curve at that point. The same definition applies to space curves and curves in n-dimensional Euclidean space.

a. Tangent line	b. Minimal surface
c. Lie derivative	d. Sphere

15. The first Frenet vector $e_1(t)$ is the _____ in the same direction, defined at each regular point of γ:

$$\mathbf{e}_1(t) = \frac{\gamma'(t)}{\|\gamma'(t)\|}.$$

If t = s is the natural parameter then the tangent vector has unit length, so that the formula simplifies:

$$\mathbf{e}_1(s) = \gamma'(s).$$

The _____ determines the orientation of the curve, or the forward direction, corresponding to the increasing values of the parameter.

The normal vector, sometimes called the curvature vector, indicates the deviance of the curve from being a straight line.

It is defined as

$$\overline{\mathbf{e}_2}(t) = \gamma''(t) - \langle \gamma''(t), \mathbf{e}_1(t) \rangle \, \mathbf{e}_1(t).$$

Its normalized form, the unit normal vector, is the second Frenet vector $e_2(t)$ and defined as

$$\mathbf{e}_2(t) = \frac{\overline{\mathbf{e}_2}(t)}{\|\overline{\mathbf{e}_2}(t)\|}.$$

The tangent and the normal vector at point t define the osculating plane at point t.

a. Isothermal coordinates	b. ACTRAN
c. Invariant differential operator	d. Unit tangent vector

16. Let f be a differentiable function, and let f'(x) be its derivative. The derivative of f'(x) (if it has one) is written f''(x) and is called the _____ of f. Similarly, the derivative of a _____, if it exists, is written f'''(x) and is called the third derivative of f.

a. Ramp function
b. Horizontal asymptote
c. Second derivative
d. Stationary phase approximation

17. A _____ is a type of manifold that is locally similar enough to Euclidean space to allow one to do calculus Any manifold can be described by a collection of charts, also known as an atlas.
   a. Lie derivative
   b. Minimal surface
   c. Tortuosity
   d. Differentiable manifold

18. In mathematics, a _____ is a series with a constant ratio between successive terms. For example, the series

$$\frac{1}{2} + \frac{1}{4} + \frac{1}{8} + \frac{1}{16} + \cdots$$

is geometric, because each term is equal to half of the previous term. The sum of this series is 1, as illustrated in the following picture:

_____ are one of the simplest examples of infinite series with finite sums.

   a. Telescoping series
   b. Converge absolutely
   c. Geometric series
   d. Sequence transformation

19. For some curves there is a smallest number L that is an upper bound on the length of any polygonal approximation. If such a number exists, then the curve is said to be rectifiable and the curve is defined to have _____ L.

Let C be a curve in Euclidean (or, generally, a metric) space X = R^n, so C is the image of a continuous function f : [a, b] → X of the interval [a, b] into X.

   a. Order of integration
   b. Integration by parametric derivatives
   c. Integrand
   d. Arc length

20. In mathematics, _____ refers to any of a number of loosely related concepts in different areas of geometry. Intuitively, _____ is the amount by which a geometric object deviates from being flat, or straight in the case of a line, but this is defined in different ways depending on the context. There is a key distinction between extrinsic _____, which is defined for objects embedded in another space (usually a Euclidean space) in a way that relates to the radius of _____ of circles that touch the object, and intrinsic _____, which is defined at each point in a differential manifold.
   a. Tortuosity
   b. Lie derivative
   c. Tangent line
   d. Curvature

21. A surface normal to a flat surface is a vector which is perpendicular to that surface. A normal to a non-flat surface at a point P on the surface is a vector perpendicular to the tangent plane to that surface at P. The word 'normal' is also used as an adjective: a line normal to a plane, the normal component of a force, the _____, etc. The concept of normality generalizes to orthogonality.
   a. PDE surfaces
   b. Paraboloid
   c. Hyperbolic paraboloid
   d. Normal vector

Chapter 10. Vector Functions

22. In mathematics, a _____ in a normed vector space is a vector (often a spatial vector) whose length is 1 (the unit length.) A _____ is often denoted by a lowercase letter with a superscribed caret or e;hate;, like this: $\hat{\imath}$.

In Euclidean space, the dot product of two unit vectors is simply the cosine of the angle between them.

    a. Overdetermined   b. ACTRAN
    c. ALGOR   d. Unit vector

23. In physics, _____ is defined as the rate of change of position. it is vector physical quantity; both speed and direction are required to define it. In the SI (metric) system, it is measured in meters per second: (m/s) or ms^{-1}.
    a. Velocity   b. BDDC
    c. BIBO stability   d. 15 theorem

24. In physics, and more specifically kinematics, _____ is the change in velocity over time. Because velocity is a vector, it can change in two ways: a change in magnitude and/or a change in direction. In one dimension, _____ is the rate at which something speeds up or slows down.
    a. ACTRAN   b. AUSM
    c. ALGOR   d. Acceleration

25. A _____ is the path a moving object follows through space. The object might be a projectile or a satellite, for example. It thus includes the meaning of orbit - the path of a planet, an asteroid or a comet as it travels around a central mass.
    a. BIBO stability   b. BDDC
    c. 15 theorem   d. Trajectory

26. _____ was a German mathematician, astronomer and astrologer, and key figure in the 17th century scientific revolution. He is best known for his eponymous laws of planetary motion, codified by later astronomers based on his works Astronomia nova, Harmonices Mundi, and Epitome of Copernican Astronomy. They also provided one of the foundations for Isaac Newton's theory of universal gravitation.
    a. Johannes Kepler   b. Robin K. Bullough
    c. MÄ dhava of Sangamagrama d. Nicolaus Copernicus

27. _____ is a PDE solver of Maxwell's equations based on the method of moments. It is a 3-D planar electromagnetic (EM) simulator used for passive circuit analysis. It is presently marketed by Agilent Technologies EEsof division , but the tool was original developed by a Belgian company, Alphabit, a spinoff from IMEC, which was acquired by Hewlett-Packard and later spun out as part of Agilent.
    a. Partial Element Equivalent Circuit   b. Trefftz method
    c. Stencil   d. Momentum

28. A _____ is a surface in the Euclidean space R^3 which is defined by a parametric equation with two parameters. Parametric representation is the most general way to specify a surface. Surfaces that occur in two of the main theorems of vector calculus, Stokes' theorem and divergence theorem, are frequently given in a parametric form.
    a. Parametric surface   b. Normal line
    c. Paraboloid   d. PDE surfaces

29. A _____ is a surface created by rotating a curve lying on some plane (the generatrix) around a straight line (the axis of rotation) that lies on the same plane.

Examples of surfaces generated by a straight line are the cylindrical and conical surfaces. A circle that is rotated about a (coplanar) axis through the center generates a sphere.

- a. Disk integration
- b. Nonelementary integral
- c. Solid of revolution
- d. Surface of revolution

30. In geometry, a _____ (pl. tori) is a surface of revolution generated by revolving a circle in three dimensional space about an axis coplanar with the circle, which does not touch the circle. Examples of tori include the surfaces of doughnuts and inner tubes.

- a. Prolate
- b. PDE surfaces
- c. Normal vector
- d. Torus

Chapter 11. Partial Derivatives

1. In mathematics, a _____ is an ordered list of objects (or events). Like a set, it contains members (also called elements or terms), and the number of terms (possibly infinite) is called the length of the _____. Unlike a set, order matters, and the exact same elements can appear multiple times at different positions in the _____.

   a. Sequence
   b. Y-intercept
   c. BDDC
   d. 15 theorem

2. In economics, the _____ functional form of production functions is widely used to represent the relationship of an output to inputs. It was proposed by Knut Wicksell (1851-1926), and tested against statistical evidence by Charles Cobb and Paul Douglas in 1900-1928.

For production, the function is

$$Y = AL^{\alpha}K^{\beta},$$

where:

- Y = total production (the monetary value of all goods produced in a year)
- L = labor input
- K = capital input
- A = total factor productivity
- α and β are the output elasticities of labor and capital, respectively. These values are constants determined by available technology.

Output elasticity measures the responsiveness of output to a change in levels of either labor or capital used in production, ceteris paribus. For example if α = 0.15, a 1% increase in labor would lead to approximately a 0.15% increase in output.

   a. BIBO stability
   b. BDDC
   c. Cobb-Douglas
   d. 15 theorem

3. A _____ or Gompertz function, named after Benjamin Gompertz, is a sigmoid function. It is a type of mathematical model for a time series, where growth is slowest at the start and end of a time period. Graphs of Gompertz curves, showing the effect of varying one of a,b,c while keeping the others constant.

$$y(t) = ae^{be^{ct}}$$

where

- a is the upper asymptote
- c is the growth rate
- b, c are negative numbers
- e is Euler's Number (e = 2.71828...)

The function curve can be derived from Gompertz's law, which states the rate of mortality (decay) falls exponentially with current size. Mathematically

$$k^r \propto \frac{1}{y(t)}$$

where

- $r = \dfrac{y'(t)}{y(t)}$ is the rate of growth.
- k is an arbitrary constant.

Examples of uses for Gompertz curves include:

- Mobile phone uptake, where costs were initially high (so uptake was slow), followed by a period of rapid growth, followed by a slowing of uptake as saturation was reached.
- Population in a confined space, as birth rates first increase and then slow as resource limits are reached.
- Modeling of growth of tumors

In the sixties A.K. Laird for the first time successfully used the _____ to fit data of growth of tumors. In fact, tumors are cellular populations growing in a confined space where the availability of nutrients is limited.

a. Neumann-Dirichlet method
b. Spheroidal wave functions
c. Duffing equation
d. Gompertz curve

4. In geometry, a _____ is a special plane curve generated by the trace of a fixed point on a small circle that rolls within a larger circle. It is comparable to the cycloid but instead of the circle rolling along a line, it rolls within a circle. The red curve is a _____ traced as the smaller black circle rolls around inside the larger blue circle (parameters are R=3.0, r=1.0, and so k=3), giving a deltoid.

If the smaller circle has radius r, and the larger circle has radius R = kr, then the parametric equations for the curve can be given by either:

$$x(\theta) = (R - r)\cos\theta + r\cos\left(\frac{R-r}{r}\theta\right)$$
$$y(\theta) = (R - r)\sin\theta - r\sin\left(\frac{R-r}{r}\theta\right),$$

or:

$$x(\theta) = r(k-1)\cos\theta + r\cos((k-1)\theta)$$
$$y(\theta) = r(k-1)\sin\theta - r\sin((k-1)\theta).$$

If k is an integer, then the curve is closed, and has k cusps (i.e., sharp corners, where the curve is not differentiable.)

- a. Bullet-nose curve
- b. Kappa curve
- c. Closed curve
- d. Hypocycloid

5. An _____ process is a change in which the temperature of the system stays constant: ΔT = 0. This typically occurs when a system is in contact with an outside thermal reservoir (heat bath), and the change occurs slowly enough to allow the system to continually adjust to the temperature of the reservoir through heat exchange. An alternative special case in which a system exchanges no heat with its surroundings (Q = 0) is called an adiabatic process.

- a. Isothermal
- b. ALGOR
- c. AUSM
- d. ACTRAN

6. In calculus and other branches of mathematical analysis, an _____ is an algebraic expression obtained in the context of limits. Limits involving algebraic operations are often performed by replacing subexpressions by their limits; if the expression obtained after this substitution does not give enough information to determine the original limit, it is known as an _____. The indeterminate forms include 0^0, $0/0$, 1^∞, $\infty - \infty$, ∞/∞, $0\times\infty$, and ∞^0.

- a. ALGOR
- b. Indeterminate form
- c. AUSM
- d. ACTRAN

7. In mathematics, the concept of a '_____' is used to describe the behavior of a function as its argument or input either 'gets close' to some point, or as the argument becomes arbitrarily large; or the behavior of a sequence's elements as their index increases indefinitely. Limits are used in calculus and other branches of mathematical analysis to define derivatives and continuity.

In formulas, _____ is usually abbreviated as lim

- a. Limit
- b. BDDC
- c. 15 theorem
- d. BIBO stability

8. _____ or isopotential in mathematics and physics (especially electronics) refers to a region in space where every point in it is at the same potential. This usually refers to a scalar potential, although it can also be applied to vector potentials. Often, _____ surfaces are used to visualize an (n)-dimensional scalar potential function in (n-1) dimensional space.

- a. Inverse function theorem
- b. Implicit function theorem
- c. Upper convected time derivative
- d. Equipotential

Chapter 11. Partial Derivatives

9. In mathematics, a (topological) _____ is defined as follows: let I be an interval of real numbers (i.e. a non-empty connected subset of $\mathbb{R}$); then a _____ γ is a continuous mapping $\gamma : I \to X$, where X is a topological space. The _____ γ is said to be simple if it is injective, i.e. if for all x, y in I, we have $\gamma(x) = \gamma(y) \implies x = y$. If I is a closed bounded interval $[a, b]$, we also allow the possibility $\gamma(a) = \gamma(b)$ (this convention makes it possible to talk about closed simple _____.)

   a. Closed curve
   b. Tractrix
   c. Prolate cycloid
   d. Curve

10. In vector calculus, the _____ is shorthand for either the _____ matrix or its determinant, the _____ determinant.

In algebraic geometry the _____ of a curve means the _____ variety: a group variety associated to the curve, in which the curve can be embedded.

These concepts are all named after the mathematician Carl Gustav Jacob Jacobi.

   a. Symmetry of second derivatives
   b. Partial derivative
   c. Contact
   d. Jacobian

11. In mathematics, a _____ is any function which can be written as the ratio of two polynomial functions.

$$y = \frac{x^2 - 3x - 2}{x^2 - 4}$$

In the case of one variable, x, a _____ is a function of the form

$$f(x) = \frac{P(x)}{Q(x)}$$

where P and Q are polynomial function in x and Q is not the zero polynomial. The domain of f is the set of all points x for which the denominator Q(x) is not zero.

   a. 15 theorem
   b. BDDC
   c. Rational function
   d. BIBO stability

12. In calculus, a branch of mathematics, the _____ is a measurement of how a function changes when its input changes. Loosely speaking, a _____ can be thought of as how much a quantity is changing at some given point. For example, the _____ of the position (or distance) of a vehicle with respect to time is the instantaneous velocity (respectively, instantaneous speed) at which the vehicle is traveling.

The process of finding a _____ is called differentiation. The fundamental theorem of calculus states that differentiation is the reverse process to integration.

Chapter 11. Partial Derivatives

a. Mountain pass theorem
b. Ramp function
c. Concave upwards
d. Derivative

13. In mathematics, a _____ of a function of several variables is its derivative with respect to one of those variables with the others held constant (as opposed to the total derivative, in which all variables are allowed to vary.) Partial derivatives are useful in vector calculus and differential geometry.

The _____ of a function f with respect to the variable x is written as f '$_x$, ∂_xf, or ∂f/∂x.

a. Monkey saddle
b. Shift theorem
c. Second partial derivatives test
d. Partial derivative

14. In infinitesimal calculus, a _____ is traditionally an infinitesimally small change in a variable. For example, if x is a variable, then a change in the value of x is often denoted Δx (or δx when this change is considered to be small.) The _____ dx represents such a change, but is infinitely small.

a. Related rates
b. Continuous function
c. Dirichlet integral
d. Differential

15. A _____ is a mathematical equation for an unknown function of one or several variables that relates the values of the function itself and of its derivatives of various orders. they play a prominent role in engineering, physics, economics and other disciplines.

A simplified real world example of a _____ is modeling the acceleration of a ball falling through the air (considering only gravity and air resistance.)

a. Lax pair
b. Structural stability
c. Petrovsky lacuna
d. Differential equation

16. In acoustics and telecommunication, a _____ of a wave is a component frequency of the signal that is an integer multiple of the fundamental frequency. For example, if the fundamental frequency is f, the harmonics have frequencies f, 2f, 3f, 4f, etc. The harmonics have the property that they are all periodic at the fundamental frequency, therefore the sum of harmonics is also periodic at that frequency.

a. 15 theorem
b. BIBO stability
c. Harmonic
d. BDDC

17. In mathematics, mathematical physics and the theory of stochastic processes, a _____ is a twice continuously differentiable function f : U → R (where U is an open subset of R^n) which satisfies Laplace's equation, i.e.

$$\frac{\partial^2 f}{\partial x_1^2} + \frac{\partial^2 f}{\partial x_2^2} + \cdots + \frac{\partial^2 f}{\partial x_n^2} = 0$$

everywhere on U. This is also often written as

$$\nabla^2 f = 0 \quad \text{or} \quad \Delta f = 0.$$

There also exists a seemingly weaker definition that is equivalent. Indeed a function is harmonic if and only if it is weakly harmonic.

Harmonic functions can be defined on an arbitrary Riemannian manifold, using the Laplace-de Rham operator Δ.

a. Newtonian potential
b. Maximum principle
c. Hilbert transform
d. Harmonic function

18. The _____ are a pair of first order, non-linear, differential equations frequently used to describe the dynamics of biological systems in which two species interact, one a predator and one its prey. They were proposed independently by Alfred J. Lotka in 1925 and Vito Volterra in 1926.

where

- y is the number of some predator;
- x is the number of its prey;
- dy/dt and dx/dt represents the growth of the two populations against time;
- t represents the time; and
- >α, >β, >γ and >δ are parameters representing the interaction of the two species.

When multiplied out, the equations take a form useful for physical interpretation. Their origin should be considered from a more general framework,

where both functions represent per capita growth rates of the prey and predator, respectively.

a. BIBO stability
b. Lotka-Volterra equations
c. 15 theorem
d. BDDC

19. The _____ is an important second-order linear partial differential equation that describes the propagation of a variety of waves, such as sound waves, light waves and water waves. It arises in fields such as acoustics, electromagnetics, and fluid dynamics. Historically, the problem of a vibrating string such as that of a musical instrument was studied by Jean le Rond d'Alembert, Leonhard Euler, Daniel Bernoulli, and Joseph-Louis Lagrange.

a. Klein-Gordon equation
c. Moment of Inertia
b. Wave equation
d. Dirac equation

20. The _____ is an important partial differential equation which describes the distribution of heat (or variation in temperature) in a given region over time. For a function u(x,y,z,t) of three spatial variables (x,y,z) and the time variable t, the _____ is

$$\frac{\partial u}{\partial t} - k\left(\frac{\partial^2 u}{\partial x^2} + \frac{\partial^2 u}{\partial y^2} + \frac{\partial^2 u}{\partial z^2}\right) = 0$$

or equivalently

$$\frac{\partial u}{\partial t} = k\nabla^2 u$$

where k is a constant.

The _____ is of fundamental importance in diverse scientific fields.

a. Heat equation
c. BIBO stability
b. 15 theorem
d. BDDC

21. In mathematics, a _____ is an approximation of a general function using a linear function (more precisely, an affine function.)

Given a differentiable function f of one real variable, Taylor's theorem for n=1 states that

$$f(x) = f(a) + f\,'(a)(x-a) + R_2$$

where R_2 is the remainder term. The _____ is obtained by dropping the remainder:

$$f(x) \approx f(a) + f\,'(a)(x-a)$$

which is true for x close to a.

a. Smooth function
c. Differentiation of trigonometric functions
b. Linearity of differentiation
d. Linear approximation

22. In geometry, the _____ (or simply the tangent) to a curve at a given point is the straight line that 'just touches' the curve at that point (in the sense explained more precisely below.) As it passes through the point of tangency, the _____ is 'going in the same direction' as the curve, and in this sense it is the best straight-line approximation to the curve at that point. The same definition applies to space curves and curves in n-dimensional Euclidean space.

a. Tangent line
c. Minimal surface
b. Sphere
d. Lie derivative

23. In mathematics and its applications, _____ refers to finding the linear approximation to a function at a given point. In the study of dynamical systems, _____ is a method for assessing the local stability of an equilibrium point of a system of nonlinear differential equations or discrete dynamical systems. This method is used in fields such as engineering, physics, economics, and ecology.
    a. Point of inflection
    c. Stationary point
    b. Symmetrically continuous
    d. Linearization

24. A _____ is a surface in the Euclidean space R^3 which is defined by a parametric equation with two parameters. Parametric representation is the most general way to specify a surface. Surfaces that occur in two of the main theorems of vector calculus, Stokes' theorem and divergence theorem, are frequently given in a parametric form.
    a. Paraboloid
    c. Normal line
    b. Parametric surface
    d. PDE surfaces

25. In mathematics, a _____ is a basic technique used to simplify problems in which the original variables are replaced with new ones; the new and old variables being related in some specified way. The intent is that the problem expressed in new variables may be simpler, or else equivalent to a better understood problem.

A very simple example of a useful variable change can be seen in the problem of finding the roots of the eighth order polynomial:

$$x^8 + 3x^4 + 2 = 0$$

Eighth order polynomial equations are generally impossible to solve in terms of elementary functions.

   a. BDDC
   c. 15 theorem
   b. Cubic function
   d. Change of variables

26. Just as the definite integral of a positive function of one variable represents the area of the region between the graph of the function and the x-axis, the _____ of a positive function of two variables represents the volume of the region between the surface defined by the function (on the three dimensional Cartesian plane where z = f(x,y)) and the plane which contains its domain. (Note that the same volume can be obtained via the triple integral -- the integral of a function in three variables -- of the constant function f(x, y, z) = 1 over the above-mentioned region between the surface and the plane.) If there are more variables, a multiple integral will yield hypervolumes of multi-dimensional functions.
    a. Linearity of integration
    c. Double integral
    b. Nonelementary integral
    d. Sum rule in integration

27. Integration is an important concept in mathematics, specifically in the field of calculus and, more broadly, mathematical analysis. Given a function f of a real variable x and an interval [a, b] of the real line, the _____

$$\int_a^b f(x)\,dx,$$

is defined informally to be the net signed area of the region in the xy-plane bounded by the graph of f, the x-axis, and the vertical lines x = a and x = b.

The term '_____' may also refer to the notion of antiderivative, a function F whose derivative is the given function f.

- a. Integrand
- b. Integral
- c. Integral test for convergence
- d. Indefinite integral

28. The terms '_____' and 'independent variable' are used in similar but subtly different ways in mathematics and statistics as part of the standard terminology in those subjects. They are used to distinguish between two types of quantities being considered, separating them into those available at the start of a process and those being created by it, where the latter (dependent variables) are dependent on the former (independent variables.)

In traditional calculus, a function is defined as a relation between two terms called variables because their values vary.

- a. BIBO stability
- b. Dependent variable
- c. BDDC
- d. 15 theorem

29. The terms 'dependent variable' and '_____' are used in similar but subtly different ways in mathematics and statistics as part of the standard terminology in those subjects. They are used to distinguish between two types of quantities being considered, separating them into those available at the start of a process and those being created by it, where the latter (dependent variables) are dependent on the former (independent variables.)

In traditional calculus, a function is defined as a relation between two terms called variables because their values vary.

- a. Independent variable
- b. ALGOR
- c. ACTRAN
- d. AUSM

30. In calculus, a method called _____ can be applied to implicitly defined functions. This method is an application of the chain rule allowing one to calculate the derivative of a function given implicitly.

As explained in the introduction, y can be given as a function of x implicitly rather than explicitly. When we have an equation R (x,y) = 0, we may be able to solve it for y and then differentiate. However, sometimes it is simpler to differentiate R(x,y) with respect to x and then solve for dy / dx.

- a. Implicit function
- b. Ordinary differential equation
- c. Automatic differentiation
- d. Implicit differentiation

31. In mathematics, an _____ is a generalization for the concept of a function in which the dependent variable has not been given 'explicitly' in terms of the independent variable. To give a function f explicitly is to provide a prescription for determining the output value of the function y in terms of the input value x:

$$y = f(x.)$$

By contrast, the function is implicit if the value of y is obtained from x by solving an equation of the form:

$$R(x,y) = 0.$$

a. Ordinary differential equation
b. Automatic differentiation
c. Implicit differentiation
d. Implicit Function

32. In the branch of mathematics called multivariable calculus, the _____ is a tool which allows relations to be converted to functions. It does this by representing the relation as the graph of a function. There may not be a single function whose graph is the entire relation, but there may be such a function on a restriction of the domain of the relation.

a. Inverse function theorem
b. Upper convected time derivative
c. Isoperimetric inequality
d. Implicit Function Theorem

33. In mathematics, the _____ of a multivariate differentiable function along a given vector V at a given point P intuitively represents the instantaneous rate of change of the function, moving through P, in the direction of V. It therefore generalizes the notion of a partial derivative, in which the direction is always taken parallel to one of the coordinate axes.

The _____ is a special case of the Gâteaux derivative.

The _____ of a scalar function $f(\vec{x}) = f(x_1, x_2, \ldots, x_n)$ along a vector $\vec{v} = (v_1, \ldots, v_n)$ is the function defined by the limit

<_____>
$$\nabla_{\vec{v}} f(\vec{x}) = \lim_{h \to 0} \frac{f(\vec{x} + h\vec{v}) - f(\vec{x})}{h}.$$

Sometimes authors write D_v instead of ∇_v.

a. Directional derivative
b. Difference quotient
c. Symmetric derivative
d. Reduced derivative

34. In vector calculus, the _____ of a scalar field is a vector field which points in the direction of the greatest rate of increase of the scalar field, and whose magnitude is the greatest rate of change.

A generalization of the _____ for functions on a Euclidean space which have values in another Euclidean space is the Jacobian. A further generalization for a function from one Banach space to another is the Fréchet derivative.

a. Parametric derivative
b. Gradient
c. Leibniz's notation
d. Smooth function

Chapter 11. Partial Derivatives

35. In vector calculus, _____ is a vector differential operator represented by the nabla symbol: ∇.

_____ is a mathematical tool serving primarily as a convention for mathematical notation; it makes many equations easier to comprehend, write, and remember. Depending on the way _____ is applied, it can describe the gradient (slope), divergence (degree to which something converges or diverges) or curl (rotational motion at points in a fluid.)

a. Divergence Theorem
b. Del
c. Gradient theorem
d. Divergence

36. In the two-dimensional case, a _____ perpendicularly intersects the tangent line to a curve at a given point.

The _____ is often used in computer graphics to determine a surface's orientation toward a light source for flat shading, or the orientation of each of the corners (vertices) to mimic a curved surface with Phong shading.

For a polygon (such as a triangle), a surface normal can be calculated as the vector cross product of two (non-parallel) edges of the polygon.

a. Parametric surface
b. Prolate
c. Normal line
d. PDE surfaces

37. The _____ is a doubly ruled surface shaped like a saddle. In a suitable coordinate system, it can be represented by the equation

$$z = \frac{x^2}{a^2} - \frac{y^2}{b^2}.$$

This is a _____ that opens up along the x-axis and down along the y-axis.

Paraboloid of revolution

With a = b an elliptic paraboloid is a paraboloid of revolution: a surface obtained by revolving a parabola around its axis.

a. Hyperbolic paraboloid
b. Parametric surface
c. PDE surfaces
d. Prolate

38. In mathematics, a _____ is a quadric surface of special kind. There are two kinds of paraboloids: elliptic and hyperbolic. The elliptic _____ is shaped like an oval cup and can have a maximum or minimum point.

a. Paraboloid
b. Normal line
c. Parametric surface
d. Normal vector

39. In mathematics, two vectors are _____ if they are perpendicular, i.e., they form a right angle. For example, a subway and the street above, although they do not physically intersect, are _____ if they cross at a right angle.

a. AUSM
b. ACTRAN
c. Orthogonal
d. ALGOR

40. In mathematics, a _____ (or critical number) is a point on the domain of a function where:

- one dimension: the derivative (or slope of the line when visualized) is equal to zero or a point where the function ceases to be differentiable.
- in general: there are two distinct concepts: either the derivative (Jacobian) vanishes, or it is not of full rank (or, in either case, the function is not differentiable); these agree in one dimension.

Note that in one dimension, a critical value or critical number x of function f is the domain element at which the derivative is zero or undefined, whereas the associated ordered pair (x, y) is the _____. In higher dimensions a critical value is in the range whereas a _____ is in the domain.

There are two situations in which a point becomes a _____ of a function of one variable. The first of which is that the value of the first derivative is equal to zero.

a. Shift theorem
b. Differentiation operator
c. Differential operator
d. Critical point

41. In a totally ordered set all elements are mutually comparable, so such a set can have at most one minimal element and at most one maximal element. Then, due to mutual comparability, the minimal element will also be the least element and the maximal element will also be the greatest element. Thus in a totally ordered set we can simply use the terms minimum and _____.

a. Dirichlet integral
b. Complex analysis
c. Maximum
d. Hyperbolic angle

42. In a totally ordered set all elements are mutually comparable, so such a set can have at most one minimal element and at most one maximal element. Then, due to mutual comparability, the minimal element will also be the least element and the maximal element will also be the greatest element. Thus in a totally ordered set we can simply use the terms _____ and maximum.

a. Taylor's theorem
b. Periodic function
c. Calculus controversy
d. Minimum

43. In mathematics, a _____ is a point in the domain of a function of two variables which is a stationary point but not a local extremum. At such a point, in general, the surface resembles a saddle that curves up in one direction, and curves down in a different direction (like a mountain pass.) In terms of contour lines, a _____ can be recognized, in general, by a contour that appears to intersect itself.

a. BDDC
b. 15 theorem
c. BIBO stability
d. Saddle point

44. Let f be a differentiable function, and let f'(x) be its derivative. The derivative of f'(x) (if it has one) is written f''(x) and is called the _____ of f. Similarly, the derivative of a _____, if it exists, is written f'''(x) and is called the third derivative of f.

a. Horizontal asymptote
b. Second Derivative
c. Ramp function
d. Stationary phase approximation

45. In mathematics, a function f defined on some set X with real or complex values is a _____ function, if the set of its values is _____. In other words, there exists a number M>0 such that

$$|f(x)| \leq M$$

for all x in X.

Sometimes, if $f(x) \leq A$ for all x in X, then the function is said to be _____ above by A.

a. Bounded
b. Stationary phase approximation
c. Caccioppoli set
d. Differential calculus

46. The largest and the smallest element of a set are called extreme values, absolute extrema, or extreme records.

For a differentiable function f, if $f(x_0)$ is an _____ for the set of all values f(x), and if x_0 is in the interior of the domain of f, then x_0 is a critical point, by Fermat's theorem.

In the case of a general partial order one should not confuse a least element (smaller than all other) and a minimal element (nothing is smaller.)

a. Integration by substitution
b. Infinitesimal
c. Extreme Value
d. Extreme Value Theorem

47. In calculus, the _____ states that if a real-valued function f is continuous in the closed and bounded interval [a,b], then f must attain its maximum and minimum value, each at least once. That is, there exist numbers c and d in [a,b] such that:

$$f(c) \geq f(x) \geq f(d) \quad \text{for all } x \in [a, b].$$

A related theorem is the boundedness theorem which states that a continuous function f in the closed interval [a,b] is bounded on that interval. That is, there exist real numbers m and M such that:

$$m \leq f(x) \leq M \quad \text{for all } x \in [a, b].$$

The _____ enriches the boundedness theorem by saying that not only is the function bounded, but it also attains its least upper bound as its maximum and its greatest lower bound as its minimum.

a. Extreme Value Theorem
b. Integral of secant cubed
c. Infinitesimal
d. Uniform convergence

48. The method of _____ or ordinary _____ is used to solve overdetermined systems. _____ is often applied in statistical contexts, particularly regression analysis.

_____ can be interpreted as a method of fitting data. The best fit in the _____ sense is that instance of the model for which the sum of squared residuals has its least value, a residual being the difference between an observed value and the value given by the model.

- a. BDDC
- b. BIBO stability
- c. 15 theorem
- d. Least squares

49. In calculus, _____ gives a sequence of approximations of a differentiable function around a given point by polynomials (the Taylor polynomials of that function) whose coefficients depend only on the derivatives of the function at that point. The theorem also gives precise estimates on the size of the error in the approximation. The theorem is named after the mathematician Brook Taylor, who stated it in 1712, though the result was first discovered 41 years earlier in 1671 by James Gregory.
- a. Complex analysis
- b. Continuous function
- c. Leibniz differential
- d. Taylor's theorem

50. In mathematical optimization, the method of Lagrange multipliers provides a strategy for finding the maximum/minimum of a function subject to constraints.

For example, consider the optimization problem

$$\text{maximize } f(x, y)$$
$$\text{subject to } g(x, y) = c.$$

We introduce a new variable (λ) called a _____, and study the Lagrange function defined by

$$\Lambda(x, y, \lambda) = f(x, y) - \lambda\big(g(x, y) - c\big).$$

If (x,y)‰ is a maximum for the original constrained problem, then there exists a λ such that (x,y,λ)‰ is a stationary point for the Lagrange function (stationary points are those points where the partial derivatives of Λ are zero.) However, not all stationary points yield a solution of the original problem.

- a. Lagrange multiplier
- b. BDDC
- c. BIBO stability
- d. 15 theorem

51. In mathematics, the simplest case of _____ refers to the study of problems in which one seeks to minimize or maximize a real function by systematically choosing the values of real or integer variables from within an allowed set. This (a scalar real valued objective function) is actually a small subset of this field which comprises a large area of applied mathematics and generalizes to study of means to obtain 'best available' values of some objective function given a defined domain where the elaboration is on the types of functions and the conditions and nature of the objects in the problem domain.

The first _____ technique, which is known as steepest descent, goes back to Gauss.

a. ACTRAN
b. AUSM
c. ALGOR
d. Optimization

1. In mathematics, a _____ is a series with a constant ratio between successive terms. For example, the series

$$\frac{1}{2} + \frac{1}{4} + \frac{1}{8} + \frac{1}{16} + \cdots$$

is geometric, because each term is equal to half of the previous term. The sum of this series is 1, as illustrated in the following picture:

_____ are one of the simplest examples of infinite series with finite sums.

a. Sequence transformation
b. Converge absolutely
c. Telescoping series
d. Geometric series

2. A _____ or Gompertz function, named after Benjamin Gompertz, is a sigmoid function. It is a type of mathematical model for a time series, where growth is slowest at the start and end of a time period. Graphs of Gompertz curves, showing the effect of varying one of a,b,c while keeping the others constant.

$$y(t) = ae^{be^{ct}}$$

where

- a is the upper asymptote
- c is the growth rate
- b, c are negative numbers
- e is Euler's Number (e = 2.71828...)

The function curve can be derived from Gompertz's law, which states the rate of mortality (decay) falls exponentially with current size. Mathematically

$$k^r \propto \frac{1}{y(t)}$$

where

- $r = \dfrac{y'(t)}{y(t)}$ is the rate of growth.
- k is an arbitrary constant.

Examples of uses for Gompertz curves include:

- Mobile phone uptake, where costs were initially high (so uptake was slow), followed by a period of rapid growth, followed by a slowing of uptake as saturation was reached.
- Population in a confined space, as birth rates first increase and then slow as resource limits are reached.
- Modeling of growth of tumors

In the sixties A.K. Laird for the first time successfully used the _____ to fit data of growth of tumors. In fact, tumors are cellular populations growing in a confined space where the availability of nutrients is limited.

a. Duffing equation
c. Spheroidal wave functions
b. Neumann-Dirichlet method
d. Gompertz curve

3. Just as the definite integral of a positive function of one variable represents the area of the region between the graph of the function and the x-axis, the _____ of a positive function of two variables represents the volume of the region between the surface defined by the function (on the three dimensional Cartesian plane where z = f(x,y)) and the plane which contains its domain. (Note that the same volume can be obtained via the triple integral -- the integral of a function in three variables -- of the constant function f(x, y, z) = 1 over the above-mentioned region between the surface and the plane.) If there are more variables, a multiple integral will yield hypervolumes of multi-dimensional functions.

a. Sum rule in integration
c. Nonelementary integral
b. Double integral
d. Linearity of integration

4. Integration is an important concept in mathematics, specifically in the field of calculus and, more broadly, mathematical analysis. Given a function f of a real variable x and an interval [a, b] of the real line, the _____

$$\int_a^b f(x)\,dx,$$

is defined informally to be the net signed area of the region in the xy-plane bounded by the graph of f, the x-axis, and the vertical lines x = a and x = b.

The term '_____' may also refer to the notion of antiderivative, a function F whose derivative is the given function f.

a. Integrand
c. Integral test for convergence
b. Indefinite integral
d. Integral

5. In mathematics, a _____ is a method for approximating the total area underneath a curve on a graph, otherwise known as an integral. It may also be used to define the integration operation.

Consider a function f: D >→ R, where D is a subset of the real numbers R, and let I = [a, b] be a closed interval contained in D. A finite set of points $\{x_0, x_1, x_2, ... x_n\}$ such that $a = x_0 < x_1 < x_2 ... < x_n = b$ creates a partition

$$P = \{[x_0, x_1), [x_1, x_2), ... [x_{n-1}, x_n]\}$$

of I.

    a. Signed measure
    c. Riemann sum
    b. Surface of revolution
    d. Disk integration

6. The _____ is a type of definite integral extended to functions of more than one real variable, for example, f(x, y) or f(x, y, z.)

Introduction

Just as the definite integral of a positive function of one variable represents the area of the region between the graph of the function and the x-axis, the double integral of a positive function of two variables represents the volume of the region between the surface defined by the function (on the three dimensional Cartesian plane where z = f(x,y)) and the plane which contains its domain. (Note that the same volume can be obtained via the triple integral -- the integral of a function in three variables -- of the constant function f(x, y, z) = 1 over the above-mentioned region between the surface and the plane.)

    a. Disk integration
    c. Multiple integral
    b. Risch algorithm
    d. Constant of integration

7. In calculus, interchange of the _____ is a methodology that transforms multiple integrations of functions into other, hopefully simpler, integrals by changing the order in which the integrations are performed.

The problem for examination is evaluation of an integral of the form:

$$\iint_D dxdy\ f(x,y),$$

where D is some two-dimensional area in the xy-plane. For some functions f straightforward integration is feasible, but where that is not true, the integral can sometimes be reduced to simpler form by changing the _____.

    a. Integration by parts
    c. Indefinite integral
    b. Arc length
    d. Order of integration

8. In mathematics and its applications, a _____ system is a system for assigning an n-tuple of numbers or scalars to each point in an n-dimensional space. This concept is part of the theory of manifolds. 'Scalars' in many cases means real numbers, but, depending on context, can mean complex numbers or elements of some other commutative ring.

Chapter 12. Multiple Integrals

a. Cylindrical coordinate system
b. Spherical coordinate system
c. 15 theorem
d. Coordinate

9. In mathematics, the _____ is a two-dimensional coordinate system in which each point on a plane is determined by an angle and a distance. The _____ is especially useful in situations where the relationship between two points is most easily expressed in terms of angles and distance; in the more familiar Cartesian or rectangular coordinate system, such a relationship can only be found through trigonometric formulation.

As the coordinate system is two-dimensional, each point is determined by two polar coordinates: the radial coordinate and the angular coordinate.

a. 15 theorem
b. BIBO stability
c. Polar coordinate system
d. BDDC

10. In mathematics, a _____ is a basic technique used to simplify problems in which the original variables are replaced with new ones; the new and old variables being related in some specified way. The intent is that the problem expressed in new variables may be simpler, or else equivalent to a better understood problem.

A very simple example of a useful variable change can be seen in the problem of finding the roots of the eighth order polynomial:

$$x^8 + 3x^4 + 2 = 0$$

Eighth order polynomial equations are generally impossible to solve in terms of elementary functions.

a. BDDC
b. 15 theorem
c. Cubic function
d. Change of variables

11. The _____ of a material is defined as its mass per unit volume. The symbol of _____ is ρ '>rho.)

Mathematically:

$$d = \frac{m}{V}$$

where:

        d is the _____,
        m is the mass,
        V is the volume.

a. Density
b. BDDC
c. BIBO stability
d. 15 theorem

Chapter 12. Multiple Integrals

12. The concept of _____ in mathematics evolved from the concept of _____ in physics. The nth _____ of a real-valued function f(x) of a real variable about a value c is

$$\mu'_n = \int_{-\infty}^{\infty} (x-c)^n f(x)\, dx.$$

It is possible to define moments for random variables in a more general fashion than moments for real values. See Moments in metric spaces.

- a. Poisson distribution
- b. Standard deviation
- c. Linear regression
- d. Moment

13. _____, also called mass _____ or the angular mass, (SI units kg m^2) is a measure of an object's resistance to changes in its rotation rate. It is the rotational analog of mass. That is, it is the inertia of a rigid rotating body with respect to its rotation.
- a. Wave equation
- b. Moment of Inertia
- c. Klein-Gordon equation
- d. Dirac equation

14. In mathematics, a _____ (pdf) is a function that represents a probability distribution in terms of integrals.

Formally, a probability distribution has density f, if f is a non-negative Lebesgue-integrable function $\mathbb{R} \to \mathbb{R}$ such that the probability of the interval [a, b] is given by

$$\int_a^b f(x)\, dx$$

for any two numbers a and b. This implies that the total integral of f must be 1.

- a. BDDC
- b. BIBO stability
- c. 15 theorem
- d. Probability density function

15. In probability theory and statistics, the _____ (or expectation value or mean and for continuous random variables with a density function it is the probability density-weighted integral of the possible values.

The term '_____' can be misleading.

- a. ACTRAN
- b. ALGOR
- c. Expected value
- d. AUSM

16. In coordinate geometry, the _____ is the y-value of the point where the graph of a function or relation intercepts the y-axis of the coordinate system.

In other words, the _____ of a function is the y-value of the point at which it intersects the line x=0 (the y-axis.) Thus, if the function is specified in form y = f(x), the _____ is easy to find by calculating f.

Chapter 12. Multiple Integrals

a. BDDC
b. 15 theorem
c. Sequence
d. Y-intercept

17. A surface normal to a flat surface is a vector which is perpendicular to that surface. A normal to a non-flat surface at a point P on the surface is a vector perpendicular to the tangent plane to that surface at P. The word 'normal' is also used as an adjective: a line normal to a plane, the normal component of a force, the _____, etc. The concept of normality generalizes to orthogonality.
   a. Normal vector
   b. Hyperbolic paraboloid
   c. PDE surfaces
   d. Paraboloid

18. _____ is how much exposed area an object has. It is expressed in square units. If an object has flat faces, its _____ can be calculated by adding together the areas of its faces.
   a. Gyroid
   b. Surface area
   c. Plane curve
   d. Lipschitz domain

19. A _____ is a surface in the Euclidean space R³ which is defined by a parametric equation with two parameters. Parametric representation is the most general way to specify a surface. Surfaces that occur in two of the main theorems of vector calculus, Stokes' theorem and divergence theorem, are frequently given in a parametric form.
   a. Normal line
   b. PDE surfaces
   c. Parametric surface
   d. Paraboloid

20. A _____ is perfectly round geometrical object in three-dimensional space, such as the shape of a round ball. Like a circle in two dimensions, a perfect _____ is completely symmetrical around its center, with all points on the surface lying the same distance r from the center point. This distance r is known as the radius of the _____.
   a. Tortuosity
   b. Sphere
   c. Minimal surface
   d. Differentiable manifold

21. A _____ is a surface created by rotating a curve lying on some plane (the generatrix) around a straight line (the axis of rotation) that lies on the same plane.

Examples of surfaces generated by a straight line are the cylindrical and conical surfaces. A circle that is rotated about a (coplanar) axis through the center generates a sphere.

   a. Nonelementary integral
   b. Disk integration
   c. Solid of revolution
   d. Surface of revolution

22. In geometry, a _____ (pl. tori) is a surface of revolution generated by revolving a circle in three dimensional space about an axis coplanar with the circle, which does not touch the circle. Examples of tori include the surfaces of doughnuts and inner tubes.
   a. Prolate
   b. PDE surfaces
   c. Normal vector
   d. Torus

23. In calculus, a method called _____ can be applied to implicitly defined functions. This method is an application of the chain rule allowing one to calculate the derivative of a function given implicitly.

As explained in the introduction, y can be given as a function of x implicitly rather than explicitly. When we have an equation R (x,y) = 0, we may be able to solve it for y and then differentiate. However, sometimes it is simpler to differentiate R(x,y) with respect to x and then solve for dy / dx.

    a. Automatic differentiation
    b. Implicit differentiation
    c. Implicit function
    d. Ordinary differential equation

24. In calculus, a branch of mathematics, the _____ is a measurement of how a function changes when its input changes. Loosely speaking, a _____ can be thought of as how much a quantity is changing at some given point. For example, the _____ of the position (or distance) of a vehicle with respect to time is the instantaneous velocity (respectively, instantaneous speed) at which the vehicle is traveling.

The process of finding a _____ is called differentiation. The fundamental theorem of calculus states that differentiation is the reverse process to integration.

    a. Ramp function
    b. Concave upwards
    c. Mountain pass theorem
    d. Derivative

25. In mathematics, a function f defined on some set X with real or complex values is a _____ function, if the set of its values is _____. In other words, there exists a number M>0 such that

$$|f(x)| \leq M$$

for all x in X.

Sometimes, if $f(x) \leq A$ for all x in X, then the function is said to be _____ above by A.

    a. Bounded
    b. Stationary phase approximation
    c. Differential calculus
    d. Caccioppoli set

26. A _____ is one of the most curvilinear basic geometric shapes:It has two faces, zero vertices, and zero edges. The surface formed by the points at a fixed distance from a given straight line, the axis of the _____. The solid enclosed by this surface and by two planes perpendicular to the axis is also called a _____.

    a. 15 theorem
    b. Right circular cylinder
    c. BDDC
    d. Cylinder

27. In geometry, a _____ is a special plane curve generated by the trace of a fixed point on a small circle that rolls within a larger circle. It is comparable to the cycloid but instead of the circle rolling along a line, it rolls within a circle. The red curve is a _____ traced as the smaller black circle rolls around inside the larger blue circle (parameters are R=3.0, r=1.0, and so k=3), giving a deltoid.

Chapter 12. Multiple Integrals

If the smaller circle has radius r, and the larger circle has radius R = kr, then the parametric equations for the curve can be given by either:

$$x(\theta) = (R - r)\cos\theta + r\cos\left(\frac{R-r}{r}\theta\right)$$
$$y(\theta) = (R - r)\sin\theta - r\sin\left(\frac{R-r}{r}\theta\right),$$

or:

$$x(\theta) = r(k - 1)\cos\theta + r\cos((k-1)\theta)$$
$$y(\theta) = r(k - 1)\sin\theta - r\sin((k-1)\theta).$$

If k is an integer, then the curve is closed, and has k cusps (i.e., sharp corners, where the curve is not differentiable.)

a. Closed curve
b. Bullet-nose curve
c. Kappa curve
d. Hypocycloid

28. In vector calculus, the _____ is shorthand for either the _____ matrix or its determinant, the _____ determinant.

In algebraic geometry the _____ of a curve means the _____ variety: a group variety associated to the curve, in which the curve can be embedded.

These concepts are all named after the mathematician Carl Gustav Jacob Jacobi.

a. Contact
b. Symmetry of second derivatives
c. Partial derivative
d. Jacobian

29. An injective function is called an injection, and is also said to be a _____ function (not to be confused with _____ correspondence, i.e. a bijective function.)

A function f that is not injective is sometimes called many-to-one. (However, this terminology is also sometimes used to mean 'single-valued', i.e. each argument is mapped to at most one value.)

a. One-to-one function
b. Onto
c. Injective function
d. One-to-one

30. In mathematics, the _____ of a function y = f(x) is a function that, in some fashion, 'undoes' the effect of f The _____ of f is denoted f $^{-1}$. The statements y=f(x) and x=f $^{-1}$(y) are equivalent.

a. AUSM
b. ALGOR
c. Inverse
d. ACTRAN

Chapter 13. Vector Calculus

1. In mathematics a _____ is a construction in vector calculus which associates a vector to every point in a (locally) Euclidean space.

Vector fields are often used in physics to model, for example, the speed and direction of a moving fluid throughout space, or the strength and direction of some force, such as the magnetic or gravitational force, as it changes from point to point.

In the rigorous mathematical treatment, (tangent) vector fields are defined on manifolds as sections of a manifold's tangent bundle.

- a. Vector field
- b. 15 theorem
- c. BIBO stability
- d. BDDC

2. In mathematics and physics, a _____ associates a scalar value, which can be either mathematical in definition to every point in space. Scalar fields are often used in physics, for instance to indicate the temperature distribution throughout space or more specifically, differential geometry, the set of functions defined on a manifold define the commutative ring of functions.

- a. Shift theorem
- b. Differential operator
- c. Jacobian
- d. Scalar field

3. In physics, _____ is defined as the rate of change of position. it is vector physical quantity; both speed and direction are required to define it. In the SI (metric) system, it is measured in meters per second: (m/s) or ms^{-1}.

- a. BIBO stability
- b. BDDC
- c. Velocity
- d. 15 theorem

4. A _____, sometimes known as an energy shield, force shield typically made of energy or charged particles, that protects a person, area or object from attacks or intrusions.

A University of Washington in Seattle group has been experimenting with using a bubble of charged plasma to surround a spacecraft, contained by a fine mesh of superconducting wire. This would protect the spacecraft from interstellar radiation and some particles without needing physical shielding.

- a. Force field
- b. 15 theorem
- c. BIBO stability
- d. BDDC

5. In vector calculus, the _____ of a scalar field is a vector field which points in the direction of the greatest rate of increase of the scalar field, and whose magnitude is the greatest rate of change.

A generalization of the _____ for functions on a Euclidean space which have values in another Euclidean space is the Jacobian. A further generalization for a function from one Banach space to another is the Fréchet derivative.

- a. Leibniz's notation
- b. Gradient
- c. Smooth function
- d. Parametric derivative

6. A _____ is a model used within physics to explain how gravity exists in the universe. In its original concept, gravity was a force between point masses. Following Newton, Laplace attempted to model gravity as some kind of radiation field or fluid, and since the 19th century explanations for gravity have usually been sought in terms of a field model, rather than a point attraction.
   a. BIBO stability
   b. BDDC
   c. 15 theorem
   d. Gravitational field

7. In mathematics, a (topological) _____ is defined as follows: let I be an interval of real numbers (i.e. a non-empty connected subset of $\mathbb{R}$); then a _____ γ is a continuous mapping $\gamma : I \to X$, where X is a topological space. The _____ γ is said to be simple if it is injective, i.e. if for all x, y in I, we have $\gamma(x) = \gamma(y) \implies x = y$. If I is a closed bounded interval $[a, b]$, we also allow the possibility $\gamma(a) = \gamma(b)$ (this convention makes it possible to talk about closed simple _____.)
   a. Prolate cycloid
   b. Tractrix
   c. Curve
   d. Closed curve

8. A _____ is a type of manifold that is locally similar enough to Euclidean space to allow one to do calculus Any manifold can be described by a collection of charts, also known as an atlas.
   a. Differentiable manifold
   b. Tortuosity
   c. Lie derivative
   d. Minimal surface

9. In mathematics, an _____ on a real vector space is a choice of which ordered bases are 'positively' oriented and which are 'negatively' oriented. In the three-dimensional Euclidean space, the two possible basis orientations are called right-handed and left-handed (or right-chiral and left-chiral), respectively. However, the choice of _____ is independent of the handedness or chirality of the bases (although right-handed bases are typically declared to be positively oriented, they may also be assigned a negative _____.)
   a. Unit vector
   b. ALGOR
   c. ACTRAN
   d. Orientation

10. The concept of _____ in mathematics evolved from the concept of _____ in physics. The nth _____ of a real-valued function f(x) of a real variable about a value c is

$$\mu'_n = \int_{-\infty}^{\infty} (x - c)^n f(x)\, dx.$$

It is possible to define moments for random variables in a more general fashion than moments for real values. See Moments in metric spaces.

   a. Standard deviation
   b. Poisson distribution
   c. Linear regression
   d. Moment

11. _____, also called mass _____ or the angular mass, (SI units kg m^2) is a measure of an object's resistance to changes in its rotation rate. It is the rotational analog of mass. That is, it is the inertia of a rigid rotating body with respect to its rotation.

a. Moment of Inertia
b. Dirac equation
c. Wave equation
d. Klein-Gordon equation

12. In mathematics, in the field of differential equations, an initial value problem is an ordinary differential equation together with specified value, called the _____, of the unknown function at a given point in the domain of the solution. In physics or other sciences, modeling a system frequently amounts to solving an initial value problem; in this context, the differential equation is an evolution equation specifying how, given initial conditions, the system will evolve with time.

An initial value problem is a differential equation

$$y'(t) = f(t, y(t)) \quad \text{with} \quad f : \mathbb{R} \times \mathbb{R} \to \mathbb{R}$$

together with a point in the domain of f

$$(t_0, y_0) \in \mathbb{R} \times \mathbb{R},$$

called the _____.

a. AUSM
b. ALGOR
c. ACTRAN
d. Initial condition

13. Integration is an important concept in mathematics, specifically in the field of calculus and, more broadly, mathematical analysis. Given a function f of a real variable x and an interval [a, b] of the real line, the _____

$$\int_a^b f(x)\, dx,$$

is defined informally to be the net signed area of the region in the xy-plane bounded by the graph of f, the x-axis, and the vertical lines x = a and x = b.

The term '_____' may also refer to the notion of antiderivative, a function F whose derivative is the given function f.

a. Integral test for convergence
b. Integral
c. Integrand
d. Indefinite integral

14. A curve γ is said to be closed or a loop if $I = [a, b]$ and if $\gamma(a) = \gamma(b)$. A _____ is thus a continuous mapping of the circle S^1; a simple _____ is also called a Jordan curve or a Jordan arc. The Jordan curve theorem states that such curves divide the plane into an 'interior' and an 'exterior'.

a. Bullet-nose curve
b. Curve
c. Kappa curve
d. Closed Curve

Chapter 13. Vector Calculus

15. In metric topology and related fields of mathematics, a set U is called _____ if, intuitively speaking, starting from any point x in U one can move by a small amount in any direction and still be in the set U. In other words, the distance between any point x in U and the edge of U is always greater than zero.

As an example, consider the _____ interval (0, 1) consisting of all real numbers x with 0 < x < 1. Here, the topology is the usual topology on the real line. We can look at this in two ways.

    a. AUSM   b. Open
    c. ALGOR   d. ACTRAN

16. The _____ of an object is the extra energy which it possesses due to its motion. It is defined as the work needed to accelerate a body of a given mass from rest to its current velocity. Having gained this energy during its acceleration, the body maintains this _____ unless its speed changes.
    a. 15 theorem   b. BDDC
    c. Potential energy   d. Kinetic energy

17. The _____ states that the total amount of energy in an isolated system remains constant. A consequence of this law is that energy cannot be created or destroyed. The only thing that can happen with energy in an isolated system is that it can change form, that is to say for instance kinetic energy can become thermal energy.
    a. Potential energy   b. BDDC
    c. 15 theorem   d. Law of Conservation of Energy

18. _____ can be thought of as energy stored within a physical system. It is called _____ because it has the potential to be converted into other forms of energy, such as kinetic energy, and to do work in the process. The standard (SI) unit of measure for _____ is the joule, the same as for work or energy in general.
    a. BDDC   b. 15 theorem
    c. Law of Conservation of Energy   d. Potential energy

19. In vector calculus, the _____ is an operator that measures the magnitude of a vector field's source or sink at a given point; the _____ of a vector field is a (signed) scalar. For example, consider air as it is heated or cooled. The relevant vector field for this example is the velocity of the moving air at a point.
    a. Gradient theorem   b. Divergence
    c. Triple product   d. Divergence Theorem

20. In vector calculus a conservative vector field is a vector field which is the gradient of a scalar potential. There are two closely related concepts: path independence and _____ vector fields. Every conservative vector field has zero curl (and is thus _____), and every conservative vector field has the path independence property.
    a. Irrotational   b. ACTRAN
    c. AUSM   d. ALGOR

21. In mathematics and physics, the _____ or Laplacian, denoted by Δ or ∇^2 and named after Pierre-Simon de Laplace, is a differential operator, specifically an important case of an elliptic operator, with many applications. In physics, it is used in modeling of wave propagation, heat flow and forming the Helmholtz equation. It is central in electrostatics and fluid mechanics, anchoring in Laplace's equation and Poisson's equation.

a. Vector Laplacian
c. Differentiation operator
b. Partial derivative
d. Laplace operator

22. In mathematics, a _____ is an ordered list of objects (or events). Like a set, it contains members (also called elements or terms), and the number of terms (possibly infinite) is called the length of the _____. Unlike a set, order matters, and the exact same elements can appear multiple times at different positions in the _____.

a. Y-intercept
c. BDDC
b. 15 theorem
d. Sequence

23. In calculus, a branch of mathematics, the _____ is a measurement of how a function changes when its input changes. Loosely speaking, a _____ can be thought of as how much a quantity is changing at some given point. For example, the _____ of the position (or distance) of a vehicle with respect to time is the instantaneous velocity (respectively, instantaneous speed) at which the vehicle is traveling.

The process of finding a _____ is called differentiation. The fundamental theorem of calculus states that differentiation is the reverse process to integration.

a. Mountain pass theorem
c. Derivative
b. Concave upwards
d. Ramp function

24. In geometry, a _____ is a special plane curve generated by the trace of a fixed point on a small circle that rolls within a larger circle. It is comparable to the cycloid but instead of the circle rolling along a line, it rolls within a circle. The red curve is a _____ traced as the smaller black circle rolls around inside the larger blue circle (parameters are R=3.0, r=1.0, and so k=3), giving a deltoid.

If the smaller circle has radius r, and the larger circle has radius R = kr, then the parametric equations for the curve can be given by either:

$$x(\theta) = (R-r)\cos\theta + r\cos\left(\frac{R-r}{r}\theta\right)$$
$$y(\theta) = (R-r)\sin\theta - r\sin\left(\frac{R-r}{r}\theta\right),$$

or:

$$x(\theta) = r(k-1)\cos\theta + r\cos((k-1)\theta)$$
$$y(\theta) = r(k-1)\sin\theta - r\sin((k-1)\theta).$$

If k is an integer, then the curve is closed, and has k cusps (i.e., sharp corners, where the curve is not differentiable.)

a. Bullet-nose curve
c. Closed curve
b. Kappa curve
d. Hypocycloid

Chapter 13. Vector Calculus

25. A _____ is a surface in the Euclidean space R^3 which is defined by a parametric equation with two parameters. Parametric representation is the most general way to specify a surface. Surfaces that occur in two of the main theorems of vector calculus, Stokes' theorem and divergence theorem, are frequently given in a parametric form.

   a. Parametric surface   b. PDE surfaces
   c. Normal line   d. Paraboloid

26. _____ is how much exposed area an object has. It is expressed in square units. If an object has flat faces, its _____ can be calculated by adding together the areas of its faces.

   a. Plane curve   b. Gyroid
   c. Lipschitz domain   d. Surface area

27. In mathematics, a _____ is a definite integral taken over a surface (which may be a curved set in space); it can be thought of as the double integral analog of the line integral. Given a surface, one may integrate over it scalar fields (that is, functions which return numbers as values), and vector fields (that is, functions which return vectors as values.)

Surface integrals have applications in physics, particularly with the classical theory of electromagnetism.

   a. Jacobian   b. Second partial derivatives test
   c. Surface integral   d. Hessian matrix

28. In the various subfields of physics, there exist two common usages of the term _____, both with rigorous mathematical frameworks.

- In the study of transport phenomena (heat transfer, mass transfer and fluid dynamics), _____ is defined as the amount that flows through a unit area per unit time. _____ in this definition is a vector.
- In the field of electromagnetism and mathematics, _____ is usually the integral of a vector quantity over a finite surface. The result of this integration is a scalar quantity. The magnetic _____ is thus the integral of the magnetic vector field B over a surface, and the electric _____ is defined similarly. Using this definition, the _____ of the Poynting vector over a specified surface is the rate at which electromagnetic energy flows through that surface. Confusingly, the Poynting vector is sometimes called the power _____, which is an example of the first usage of _____, above. It has units of watts per square metre (WÂ·m^{-2})

One could argue, based on the work of James Clerk Maxwell, that the transport definition precedes the more recent way the term is used in electromagnetism. The specific quote from Maxwell is 'In the case of fluxes, we have to take the integral, over a surface, of the _____ through every element of the surface. The result of this operation is called the surface integral of the _____.

   a. 15 theorem   b. Flux
   c. BIBO stability   d. BDDC

29. In vector calculus, the _____ Ostrogradskye;s theorem the _____ states that the outward flux of a vector field through a surface is equal to the triple integral of the divergence on the region inside the surface. Intuitively, it states that the sum of all sources minus the sum of all sinks gives the net flow out of a region.

   a. Gradient theorem   b. Divergence Theorem
   c. Divergence   d. Triple product

ANSWER KEY

Chapter 1
1. d	2. c	3. d	4. b	5. d	6. d	7. d	8. d	9. d	10. c
11. a	12. b	13. b	14. d	15. a	16. d	17. d	18. c	19. c	20. d
21. d	22. d	23. d	24. d	25. d	26. d	27. b	28. c	29. d	30. d
31. d	32. d	33. c	34. c	35. c	36. b	37. c	38. d	39. d	40. b
41. d	42. a	43. a	44. d	45. a	46. c	47. c	48. d	49. d	50. d
51. b	52. d	53. b	54. b	55. d	56. d	57. a	58. d	59. d	60. c
61. d	62. b	63. d	64. c	65. d	66. d	67. c	68. a	69. d	70. a
71. b	72. d	73. d	74. d	75. d	76. d	77. d	78. b	79. d	

Chapter 2
1. b	2. a	3. d	4. c	5. d	6. c	7. a	8. a	9. c	10. d
11. b	12. c	13. d	14. d	15. d	16. d	17. d	18. a	19. a	20. c
21. b	22. d	23. c	24. c	25. c	26. c	27. d	28. b	29. b	30. c
31. d	32. c	33. d	34. d	35. b	36. d	37. d			

Chapter 3
1. a	2. d	3. c	4. c	5. d	6. c	7. c	8. d	9. d	10. b
11. b	12. a	13. d	14. d	15. c	16. d	17. c	18. c	19. c	20. d
21. a	22. a	23. d	24. a	25. b	26. d	27. d	28. d	29. a	30. c
31. a	32. b	33. d	34. d	35. d	36. d	37. c	38. d	39. a	40. a
41. a	42. c	43. d	44. d	45. c	46. b	47. c	48. a	49. d	50. d
51. b	52. d	53. d	54. d	55. b	56. d	57. d	58. c	59. d	60. c
61. a	62. c	63. c	64. b	65. d					

Chapter 4
1. a	2. c	3. d	4. d	5. a	6. d	7. d	8. d	9. d	10. d
11. d	12. a	13. d	14. c	15. b	16. d	17. a	18. c	19. c	20. c
21. d	22. c	23. d	24. a	25. d	26. a	27. d	28. b	29. a	

Chapter 5
1. a	2. a	3. d	4. d	5. b	6. b	7. d	8. d	9. a	10. d
11. d	12. d	13. b	14. d	15. c	16. d	17. d	18. d	19. a	20. d
21. a	22. d	23. c	24. b	25. c	26. c	27. d	28. d	29. b	30. b
31. c	32. a	33. b	34. b	35. b	36. d	37. d	38. d	39. d	40. c
41. b	42. d	43. d	44. a	45. a	46. d	47. c	48. d	49. c	50. d
51. d	52. d	53. a	54. d	55. b					

Chapter 6
1. a	2. a	3. c	4. b	5. d	6. c	7. a	8. d	9. c	10. d
11. d	12. a	13. d	14. d	15. c	16. d	17. d	18. d	19. b	20. d
21. b	22. c	23. d	24. d	25. b	26. c	27. a	28. d		

Chapter 7

1. a	2. c	3. d	4. d	5. a	6. a	7. d	8. d	9. d	10. a
11. d	12. d	13. d	14. c	15. b	16. a	17. a	18. d	19. d	20. b
21. b	22. d	23. c	24. c	25. b	26. d	27. d	28. d	29. d	

Chapter 8

1. a	2. c	3. d	4. a	5. c	6. b	7. d	8. a	9. d	10. d
11. d	12. c	13. b	14. b	15. d	16. a	17. c	18. d	19. a	20. d
21. a	22. b	23. d	24. d	25. a	26. d	27. a	28. a	29. c	30. b
31. a	32. d	33. c	34. c	35. d	36. a	37. d	38. c	39. b	40. b
41. d									

Chapter 9

1. a	2. d	3. d	4. a	5. c	6. b	7. d	8. d	9. d	10. a
11. c	12. d	13. a	14. c	15. d	16. d	17. b	18. a	19. d	20. d
21. d	22. a	23. b	24. d	25. b	26. d	27. d	28. b	29. d	30. b
31. c									

Chapter 10

1. d	2. b	3. d	4. a	5. d	6. a	7. d	8. b	9. a	10. a
11. d	12. b	13. a	14. a	15. d	16. c	17. d	18. c	19. d	20. d
21. d	22. d	23. a	24. d	25. d	26. a	27. d	28. a	29. d	30. d

Chapter 11

1. a	2. c	3. d	4. d	5. a	6. b	7. a	8. d	9. d	10. d
11. c	12. d	13. d	14. d	15. d	16. c	17. d	18. b	19. b	20. a
21. d	22. a	23. d	24. b	25. d	26. c	27. b	28. b	29. a	30. d
31. d	32. d	33. a	34. b	35. b	36. c	37. a	38. a	39. c	40. d
41. c	42. d	43. d	44. b	45. a	46. c	47. a	48. d	49. d	50. a
51. d									

Chapter 12

1. d	2. d	3. b	4. d	5. c	6. c	7. d	8. d	9. c	10. d
11. a	12. d	13. b	14. d	15. c	16. d	17. a	18. b	19. c	20. b
21. d	22. d	23. b	24. d	25. a	26. d	27. d	28. d	29. d	30. c

Chapter 13

1. a	2. d	3. c	4. a	5. b	6. d	7. c	8. a	9. d	10. d
11. a	12. d	13. b	14. d	15. b	16. d	17. d	18. d	19. b	20. a
21. d	22. d	23. c	24. d	25. a	26. d	27. c	28. b	29. b	

www.ingramcontent.com/pod-product-compliance
Lightning Source LLC
Chambersburg PA
CBHW082205230426
43672CB00015B/2912